THE ANGELIC DOCTOR

The Life and Thought of
Saint Thomas Aquinas

By

JACQUES MARITAIN

Author of "Art of Scholasticism,"
"An Introduction to Philosophy," Etc., Etc.

Translated by J. F. SCANLAN

LINCOLN MAC VEAGH

THE DIAL PRESS

NEW YORK · MCMXXXI

LONGMANS, GREEN & CO., TORONTO

MANUFACTURED IN THE UNITED STATES OF AMERICA
BY THE VAIL-BALLOU PRESS, INC., BINGHAMTON, N. Y.

DEUS, QUI ECCLESIAM TUAM BEATI
THOMAE CONFESSORIS TUI MIRA ERUDI-
TIONE CLARIFICAS, ET SANCTA OPERA-
TIONE FOECUNDAS: DA NOBIS, QUAESU-
MUS, ET QUAE DOCUIT, INTELLECTU
CONSPICERE, ET QUAE EGIT, IMITATIONE
COMPLERE. PER DOMINUM NOSTRUM
JESUM CHRISTUM, QUI TECUM VIVIT ET
REGNAT IN UNITATE SPIRITUS SANCTI,
DEUS: PER OMNIA SAECULA SAECULORUM.
AMEN. (*Missal and Breviary: Prayer for
the Feast of St. Thomas Aquinas.*)

PREFACE

THIS Essay is not an exposition of the doctrine of St. Thomas: it is an attempt rather to illustrate certain essential aspects of the personality and influence of the Angelic Doctor, of his present and ever effective influence as much as and even more than his past influence; for it is not a mediæval Thomism the author has in mind but a perennial and "actual" Thomism.

I wrote in the preface to my *Antimoderne:*

"It would argue extreme naïveté to engage in modern speculation and to sympathize with all the good it contains without first taking care to discern its spiritual principles. . . . On the contrary, once this discrimination has been made, once the constructive work which guarantees the specificity, if I may say so, of our intellectual life has been assured, then and then only may we and ought we to give free rein to the universalist tendency so admirably manifest in such as St. Thomas Aquinas, which, no less benevolent than pacific, inclines Catholic speculation to seek everywhere for concordances rather than oppositions, fragments of truth rather than privations and deviations, to preserve and adopt rather than to overturn, to build rather than to disperse. There is, to be sure, no lack of work for Catholics and plenty to tempt their spirit of initiative. For the task confronting them is one of universal integration. . . ."

Contemporary Thomist philosophy will, I hope, devote all its energies to this work of assembly and construction. A beginning had to be made by binding together again the vital cords through which wisdom continues among men, and undoing the great errors which lay like an obstacle in the way of that continuity. The truth is such criticism of error must never cease; but it is towards the future that our eyes are turned.

I do not conceal the fact that such a task has to be pursued amidst a general levity. As far as Catholics are concerned, if it is true that only too many have been reluctant, in the past fifty years especially, to understand the teaching of the Holy Ghost and Rome which asked them not to debase according to too human standards a religion which was divine, is it to be wondered at that once again only too often, when confronted with the supremely difficult task—which is nevertheless theirs—of thinking the world and the present moment in the light of eternal truths, they should have refused to go, as Leo XIII exhorted them to do, and ask the Common Doctor of the Church for the indispensable doctrinal equipment? So, by a not altogether sur-

prising phenomenon, the most insidious and active
opposition was raised against St. Thomas by a certain *intelligentsia* at once pious and frivolous.

As for quarters in which they believe that they
have freed themselves from the fetters of primary
Truth, what would be surprising is the fact that
Thomism had not been the object of a whole-hearted
aversion.

Such enmities clearly only encouraged me to be
the more insistent. They prove to what an extent
the Thomist renaissance irks, on the one hand, a
certain eclectic comfort and, on the other, everything that hates Christian culture. It has by this
time triumphed over many obstacles; it can no
longer be ignored, it can no longer be stifled, and it
finds all over the world minds eager to take an
interest in it. We know that the wisdom of St.
Thomas is running on the highways of the world
before the footsteps of God. The greater grow the
powers of illusion, the more will lovers of truth feel
drawn towards the vast light of that wisdom; *ibi
congregabuntur et aquilae.* Our whole task is to
prepare a way of approach to it. For this reason I
have said and I repeat: *Vae mihi, si non thomisti-
zavero.*

If those who are scandalized at such an expression had done me the honour of reading whatever
I have written with a little care, instead of being

carried away by too convenient simplifications, they might perhaps have understood that it is not "for the tranquillity of my own soul," but rather for the love of their souls that I thomistize; they would not allege that my one desire is to "declare illegitimate" and "annihilate" the aspirations of our time and they would not object against me what I myself believe, "that it is a question of ordering the abundance of all the desires the modern world begets, and that such desires are therefore to be reckoned with." They would realize finally, that my purpose is not "to proclaim order," but rather, to the limit of my strength and as long as my voice holds, to summon workers who will devote themselves under the guidance of the Angelic Doctor, to "make order" in accordance with the truth. In the sphere of philosophy the task has long since been begun: yet it can hardly be said to have been begun, because the work to be done is so enormous, so difficult to do. As far as I am concerned, I consider that I have done nothing as yet.

It is simply futile to depict "neo-Thomism," as certain other critics do, as a "panacea" suggested to dispense with intellectual effort and promote immobility or as intended, according to others, to assure a feeling of social security; to pretend that Thomists consider the *Summa Theologica* as "a massive, nay exclusive revelation" of every truth, and so forth. I confess to feeling some satisfaction at seeing such opponents of a philosophy I admire reduced to uttering such obvious untruths.

I would, however, take advantage of the opportunity such criticisms offer to declare once more:

There is a Thomist philosophy, there is no neo-Thomist philosophy. We make no claim to include anything of the past in the present, but to maintain in the present the "actuality" of the eternal.

Thomism does not want to return to the Middle Ages. As I wrote in the preface to *Antimoderne*:

"If I am anti-modern, it is certainly not out of personal inclination, but because the spirit of all modern things that have proceeded from the anti-Christian revolution compels me to be so, because it itself makes opposition to the human inheritance its own distinctive characteristic, because it hates and despises the past and worships itself and because I hate and despise that hatred and contempt and that spiritual impurity; but if it be a question of preserving and assimilating all the riches of being accumulated in modern times and sympathizing with the effort of the seekers after truth and desiring renovations, then there is nothing I desire more than to be ultra-modern. And in truth do not Christians implore the Holy Ghost to renew the face of the earth? Are they not expecting the life of the age to come? There will be novelties then and for everybody. I admire the art of the Cathedrals and Giotto and Angelico. But I loathe neo-Gothic

and pre-Raphaelitism. I am well aware that the
course of time is irreversible; in spite of the great
admiration I feel for the age of St. Louis, I do not
therefore want to go back to the Middle Ages, according to the ridiculous desire generously attributed to me by certain penetrating critics; my hope
is to see restored in a new world, and informing a
new matter, the spiritual principles and eternal
laws of which the civilization of the Middle Ages,
in its best periods, offers us only a particular historic
realization of a superior quality, in spite of its enormous deficiencies, but definitively over and done
with."

Thomism claims to make use of reason to distinguish truth from falsehood: it does not want to
destroy but to purify modern speculation and to
integrate all the truth that has been discovered
since the time of St. Thomas. It is an essentially
synthetic and assimilative philosophy, the only philosophy which, as a matter of fact, attempts
throughout the ages and the continents a work of
continuity and universality. It is also the only philosophy which, while rising to the knowledge of
the supra-sensible, first requires from experience
an unqualified adhesion to sensible reality. The task
which lies before it is to disengage from the enormous contribution which the experimental sciences
have accumulated in the past four centuries, a
genuine philosophy of nature—as, in quite another

sphere, to integrate the artistic treasure of modern times in a philosophy of art and beauty which shall be truly universal and at the same time comprehend the efforts being made at the present moment.[1]

Thomism belongs to no party either of the "right" or of the "left": it is not situate in space but in the spirit.

Thomism is a form of wisdom. Between it and the particular forms of culture incessant vital exchanges must be made, but it is rigorously independent in its essence of those particular forms. The Thomist philosophy, for example, has the most universal principles of æsthetics and yet it would be impossible —that is only too clear—to speak of a specifically "Thomist" literary school, "Thomist" painting, novels or poetry. So also Thomist theology integrates the great principles of Christian politics—and yet it would be impossible to speak of a "Thomist" political party. The wisdom of St. Thomas is above every particularisation. In this respect it partakes somewhat of the nature of Catholicism itself. *Nolite tangere.* Catholicism is a religion, both universal and universalist, the true religion. Thomism is a philosophy and a theology. The term "Catholic" applied to something other than this religion, and the term "Thomist" to something other than this phi-

---

[1] The author's *Art and Scholasticism* (Sheed & Ward) was an attempt to show how such a conversation might be engaged between the perennial philosophy and contemporary art.

losophy and this theology, become merely material designations, referring not to what derives essentially from Catholicism or Thomism, but to the activity in fact exercised in such and such a particular sphere by any particular Catholic or Thomist "subject." And to tell the truth, there is nothing which ought to fill us with greater apprehension than the thought that truth, divine or human, may be judged by the standard of our own limitations and errors.

To consider Thomism as a garment worn in the thirteenth century and now no longer fashionable —as though the value of a metaphysical system were to be appraised by some standard of time—is a specifically barbarous way of thinking. The mind wants us to consider only one philosophical system among many as valid—if it is true; but such a requirement does not prevent the knowledge that philosophical investigation is indefinitely progressive. (The progress of philosophy is achieved in a different way from the progress of the experimental sciences which are constantly checked and rectified by sensible verifications. The price which philosophy has to pay for its superiority is the possibility of developing in error. Two records of progress must, therefore, be kept distinct in the case of philosophy, according as it makes progress *per se* in virtue of increases of truth due to the continuity of an effort constantly maintained in the line of the true, or according as it makes progress *per accidens* in virtue of increases of truth procured in fact by the endless multiplicity of aberrant attempts which can advance in error only by draining some truth.)

It is no less puerile to appraise the value of a metaphysical system by the standard of its utility in preserving or destroying a social state. Wisdom has far different standards. Interpretations of history inspired by Marx or Sorel, by the very fact that they consider the material causality effectively operative in human affairs, can strictly speaking account for the success or failure of a philosophy in a particular social environment; they can offer no explanation of the *formal* element in such a philosophy. And when it is a question of a doctrine more or less outlined or prepared in the most ancient philosophic traditions of humanity, formed in Hellenic society in the time of Aristotle, taken up again and systematized in feudal society in the time of Thomas Aquinas, a doctrine whose spirituality passes intact through the most diverse ages, it is a particularly gross absurdity to regard it as a "defensive reaction" on the part of the bourgeois society of our time, a society based on fundamental principles far opposed to the principles of St. Thomas.

The philosophy of St. Thomas is independent in itself of the data of faith and dependent for its principles and structure on experience and reason.

It is a philosophy, nevertheless, which, while remaining absolutely distinct from, is still in vital communication with, the superior wisdom of theology and contemplation. And it is from contact with those superior forms of wisdom, as with the intellectual life of the Church, that it derives the strength to preserve among men the purity and universality peculiar to it.

The truths here recalled are admittedly elementary. For my own part, when I explain to my contemporaries the necessity of taking St. Thomas for a teacher, I know that I am there only to tell them so, not to persuade them in spite of themselves. "He that heareth, let him hear; and he that forbeareth, let him forbear." [2]

If the truth be told, at the bottom of what is usually urged against the present renaissance of the philosophy of St. Thomas, there is one single and singular prejudice; one of my critics ingenuously allowed it to appear in a reference to that "thirteenth-century author" whom they "are pleased to exalt above history." It is a question of ascertaining whether one is justified or not in admitting that there can possibly be something above history, and that there may exist supra-historical values. No! is the answer given by my critics. They are readily

[2] *Ezechiel*, iii, 27.

disposed to admit that St. Thomas was a great light, as great as you like, sublime, immense: but on condition that such a light shone once upon a time and now shines no longer; on condition that all that remains of St. Thomas is what may have been transmitted of his, from wave to wave, into the flux of the successive—the opinions, for example, at the present day, of M. Pierre Lasserre. What offends them, excites their wrath, gives them scandal, is that anyone should think that he, Thomas Aquinas, still subsists, that he dominates history, that his light, because it is spiritual, and his philosophy, because it is true, still continue with their essential grandeur and essential efficacy, to-day as in the time of St. Louis. Immersing every reality, even of a spiritual nature, in the flux of time, considering the value of the very substance of wisdom as essentially determined by time and history, they think that to acknowledge any immutability whatsoever, imposing itself unaided upon our minds, is to arrest the progress of time, to immobilize history, to claim to solidify the very flux of succession; they do not perceive that the immutability of what wisdom has once acquired is not in time, but above it, and, far from arresting the progress of history, rather accelerates its course and the progress of knowledge. Their philosophy under its dapper appearance is poverty itself, destitute of intellectuality, funda-

PREFACE

mental materialism. What I assert against it is that truth does not pass, does not flow away with history; that the spirit does not disintegrate, that there are stabilities not of inertia but of spirituality and life; intemporal values; eternal acquisitions; that time is in the eternal like a gold piece in the clutch of the hand; and that the mind is above time.

January, 1931.

CONTENTS

THE
ANGELIC
DOCTOR

I

THE SAINT

"Friar Giacomo di Viterbo, Archbishop of Naples, told me many a time that he believed, in accordance with the Faith and the Holy Ghost, that Our Saviour had sent, as doctor of truth to enlighten the world and the universal Church, first the apostle Paul, then Augustine, and lastly, in our own time, Friar Thomas, who, he believed, would have no successor until the end of time." (Testimony of Bartolommeo di Capua at the hearing of the case for the canonization of St. Thomas, 8th August, 1319.)

EARLY in the year 1225 (the most probable date),[1] Thomas, the seventh and youngest of the sons of Landulf, Count of Aquino, and Theodora of Theate (Chieti in the Abruzzi) was born in his father's castle at Roccasecca, not far from Naples. Landulf belonged to the Lombard nobility: his mother, Francesca di Suabia, was the sister of Frederick Barbarossa; Theodora was the descendant of Norman nobles. The complementary talents of

[1] This date has been established by the invaluable critical researches of Père Mandonnet, which are indispensable in reference to everything connected with the life of the Saint. Père Petitot's *Saint Thomas d'Aquin*, Mgr. M. Grabmann's *Thomas von Aquin* (Munich, 1912), the Pègues-Maquart translation of William of Tocco, the prior of the Dominican convent at Benevento, who had known Thomas at Naples in 1272–1274, and the depositions of witnesses at the hearing of the case for the canonization may also be usefully consulted.

North and South, transmitted through a dual lineage of nobility, blended in the child and produced a marvellously well-tempered body, selected to become the instrument of a mind excelling all minds in wisdom, the maker of unity. He came into the world at the beginning of a century when Christian civilization—already imperilled and in imminent danger of dissolution—was on the point of righting itself again to put forth its supreme fruit. Vast conflicts were everywhere waged but dominated in spite of everything by the order of the spirit, war, politics, poetry and religion, the duel between the Pope and the Emperor, the power of feudalism and the power of the Church, the pride of the strong, the virtues of the Saints; he came at the most lustily, most starkly human moment of mediæval humanity. His mother, who was to stop at nothing to prevent his following the will of God, was a woman of great virtue and self-denial. And while his brothers, rather than see him a mendicant religious, thought nothing of inciting him to mortal sin, his sister Theodora, Countess of San Severino, was to spend her life in works of mercy and penance and leave behind her a memory of sanctity.

One day, as his nurse was about to give him his bath, the little Tommaso snatched up a piece of parchment, which not for worlds would he leave go, and wept so copiously that he had to be bathed with his fist clenched. His mother came upon the scene and, in spite of his wailing and screaming, forced the hand open; the angelic greeting was found written upon the piece of parchment.

At the age of five he was placed as an oblate in the abbey of Monte Cassino; he persistently interrogated the monks, had only one question upon his lips: WHAT IS GOD? was his constant inquiry.

The silent child had no thought of anything but study and devotion; his desire was to consecrate himself to God. Could anything be simpler? They would make him a Benedictine. Providence itself intervened to confirm the precautions taken by his parents. By offering him in 1230 to the abbey which he had besieged and ravaged the year before with the armies of Frederick II, the Count of Aquino sealed his peace with the monks and contrived for the future an alliance with them advantageous to all concerned—even to the material interests of the Count, for the powerful monastery had rich endowments: and Thomas would be Abbot. Abbot he must be. That Benedictine vocation was a sort of State affair, gratifying alike to God, the Emperor and the family.

"No," said Thomas, "I will be a Preacher."

He was about fifteen or sixteen years old at the time. Political events had compelled his father to withdraw him at the age of fourteen from Monte Cassino, which had been once more ravaged by Frederick II. The child had therefore discarded his oblate's habit and been sent to Naples to complete his studies in the Faculty of Arts, where he soon became the wonder of all. The Dominicans, founded some twenty years earlier, had established in 1231 a public school of theology in the town, which was incorporated with the University. Thomas made their acquaintance there. All his life he retained a great affection for the observance of St. Benedict, and the impress of Benedictine spirituality remained indelibly engraved upon his heart. But now it was a question of obeying the secret voice which calls everyone by name and the taciturn boy was listening to God. An indomitable force of soul was at the origin of his sanctity.

Vocation is a supernatural mystery. Every natural explanation which may be offered relates only to accidentals, trivial in comparison with the essential motive. Was it in order to be given the duty of teaching or to spend himself in a more active life that Thomas wanted to become a Dominican? Or to escape the secular worries and soaring ambitions with which his family would have once more attempted to burden him, if he had taken the habit of St. Benedict? Was it even for love of the poverty of the Mendicant Friars, for pity of the souls to

whom the word of Our Lord had not been proclaimed, in reaction against the abuses which earthly
possessions had made rife among the black monks,
through the spell cast by a new Order whose con-
quering youth and challenging ideal (the religious
life informing intellectual activity itself so as to
make every member an apostle transmitting to
others the objects of his contemplation) exactly
answered the needs of the time? All such questions
are of secondary importance. He had asked: What
is God? He had to find an answer, to gather the
principles of wisdom together in the unity of a
doctrine destined continually to increase.

A privileged moment of history made such a synthesis possible. The day before, Christian speculation was not yet ripe; the day after, it had begun to
disintegrate. Before the grace of Christ and the
Cross, the weight of matter and the world, came to
share the divided heart of man for centuries between them, there was still time for the baptized
mind to assume and reconcile all things in the light
of Him Who is. This labour of strength, which
from a fugitive point of duration—the measure of
one individual, the labour of twenty-three years—
was destined to dominate all future time, was to be
accomplished by Thomas Aquinas. He was appointed to save the mind: it was for the sake of the
mind that he was forced to embrace the apostolic

life. There lay his task and woe betide him if he sought to avoid it! The immense future concealed in the will of God brought pressure to bear upon his soul, came upon him in the form of a very simple, but irresistibly compelling, command.

It was in vain that his family, hard put to it after their breach with the Emperor, whom Innocent IV had deposed,[2] later appealed for his help, in vain that the Pope offered him the abbacy of Monte Cassino (with permission to retain the habit of his Order)—and then the bishopric of Naples—Thomas would not yield.

It was a question at the time of defying the will of his father and mother, of affronting the wrath of his relations, who were not persons of feeble energy or easily placated. As he was to write later: "When parents are not in such dire necessity that they need the services of their children, children may adopt the religious life without the consent of their parents and even in defiance of their expressed wishes, because, once the age of puberty is over, anyone *sui juris* is entitled to please himself in the choice of a career, especially if the service of God is involved;

---

[2] Some of Thomas's brothers having taken part in the rebellion of 1246 against Frederick II, the family was forced into exile in Campagna of the Papal States. It was about this time that Rainaldo d'Aquino was tortured and put to death by order of the Emperor. St. Thomas, no doubt, had such incidents in mind when he wrote the article of the *Summa* (II–II, 12, 2), in which he asserts, in conformity with her teaching, the right of the Church to depose any prince or emperor—an eminent instance of her power to intervene in politics for the protection of spiritual interests.

it is better to obey the Father of spirits, in order
that we may have life, than those who have begotten
us in the flesh." [3]

Guided and confirmed in his vocation by the old
Friar Giovanni di San Giuliano, Thomas received
the habit in the spring of the year 1244, probably
from the hands of the Master-General, John the
Teuton, then on a visit to Naples. He was about
twenty years of age. His father had died a few
months earlier. But the Countess Theodora was to
prove that the trust of family authority, now transmitted to her, would be unfailingly observed.

She had no sooner been apprised of the event than
she dispatched a special messenger to those of her
sons who were in the field with the Emperor at Ac-
quapendente in Tuscany and ordered them, as they
respected her maternal blessing, to arrest and send
back to her under escort their young brother whom
the Preachers were causing to flee the realm. And
the fact was that John the Teuton had decided, in
order to save this *artist,* who now knew as much as
his master, from the resentment of his relatives and
to ensure his theological education, to take him at
once to the *studium generale* in Paris, where he himself was going. The Master-General, the novice and
three other Friars, making their way on foot, had
passed through Rome and were traversing Tuscany.

[3] *Sum. Theol.,* II–II, 189, 6.

As they sat by a fountain, they were set upon by armed men, and the brothers of Thomas seized him and tore him from his other brethren whom he had himself chosen. He wrapped himself so closely in his habit that they could not strip it from him; but they forced him on to a horse and rode to Roccasecca where the Countess Theodora awaited her son.[4]

One of Thomas's brothers, Rainaldo the poet—a favourite of the Emperor until the Emperor had him put to death—was in command of the troop. After travelling for a few days, they halted at the fortress of Monte San Giovanni, a fief of the Aquinas family some two or three hours' ride from Roccasecca. There or at Roccasecca itself occurred the famous incident of the temptation from which Thomas emerged with a cordon of angels. Rainaldo, an upright and honourable man in the world's account but one who lived after the fashion of the world, had contrived that supreme argument against the folly of his junior. The story is a fa-

[4] This episode, like the imprisonment at Roccasecca, has, as Père Mandonnet has shown, been the subject of romantic embroidery by the early historians. Although they may have added picturesque details to the story of the capture of Thomas by his brothers, the reality which they so embellished, the reality of the duress imposed, is nevertheless undeniable and it would be futile to attempt to attenuate the brutality of the incident. There can be no doubt that Thomas, who had lived in Naples the fashionable life of a young squire of his time, was a competent horseman and in the circumstances nothing is more probable than that, after the fight he surely put up, struggling to the utmost in order not to be deprived of his habit, he must have been forcibly compelled, as the old chronicles relate, to mount a horse.

miliar one, how the "young and pretty damsel, attired in all the blandishments of love" was introduced into the bedroom where Thomas lay asleep; how he rose and, snatching a brand, drove the temptress out and burned the sign of the cross upon the door. And thenceforth, by an angelic grace, was never troubled by any impulse of the flesh.

Confined for more than a year at Roccasecca, and there in spite of scenes and remonstrances keeping the habit and observing the Rule of his Order, Thomas read the Bible and the Master of the Sentences,[5] taught his sisters to read in Holy Writ and converted the elder, Marotta, to St. Benedict when she attempted to divert him from St. Dominic, so that ultimately his mother herself helped him, they say, to cheat the vigilance of his brothers and make good his escape. The chronicles relate that he fled through a window, like St. Paul of old. In reality, it seems not improbable that his release was decided by his family, whose political fortunes were in jeopardy and against whom the Master-General, John the Teuton, had filed a complaint in the court of Innocent IV.

From Naples he was sent once more to Paris, to the convent of St. Jacques where he made his noviciate and remained nearly three years; Albert the

---

[5] It was about this time that he composed for his old fellow students in the Faculty of Arts the two *opuscula, De Propositionibus Modalibus* and *De Fallaciis.*

Great was teaching there at the time, and, when Albert was sent to Cologne, Friar Thomas accompanied him; there under the direction of that immense genius, the "great dumb ox of Sicily" completed his studies and became a theologian.

After four years had elapsed, he left Cologne, on being appointed, at the suggestion of Master Albert, to the teaching staff of the convent of St. Jacques as *biblical bachelor* (1252–1254) and *sententiary bachelor* (1254–1256). The commentary on the four books of the Sentences was the work of these years, along with the *De Ente et Essentia,* and, probably, the commentary on the *Divine Attributes* of Denys.[6] At the age of thirty-one—four years earlier than the limit appointed by the Státues of the University and in virtue of a dispensation granted by the Pope—he was promoted to a master's degree in theology at the same time as his friend Friar Bonaventura.

The modern world is "blasé"; all values have been degraded in it to one dull level of equality by the stale use of custom. The words *master in theology* bring to our minds merely an academic degree of a

---

[6] According to Mandonnet, the commentary on the *Divine Attributes* must have been written later (about 1261). It would, however, appear from some very convincing arguments obligingly submitted to the author by Père Théry that this work dates from the youth of St. Thomas and must have been written before 1256, perhaps even at Cologne, between 1248 and 1250. Père Théry argues that it is to it that Tocco alludes in his statement that Thomas, "the dumb ox," began to *legere* when he was at Cologne.

sort and a conventional picture of the characters who wear the doctor's cap with varying kinds of success. It is the doctors' fault that a civilization, which has known them only too well, considers the doctorate, if not doctrine, alas! as but a poor thing. The very wise naïveté of the thirteenth century saw in the master's degree all that such an office signified *de jure* and in accordance with its essential form; the glance of a St. Thomas clearly perceived the spiritual reality in the function of teaching. As a master in theology, he was allotted the task by the Church of cultivating sacred wisdom in the minds of his hearers; he was thenceforth entirely at their service to co-operate with the vital function developing in them, he had power over the truth in souls, an awful power for which he would be accountable, for "to raise a doubt and not resolve it, is the same thing as to concede it: it is taking the cover off a cistern and not putting it back again." [7] Were it not for the grace of God, a man might almost faint for fear. Friar Thomas implored God in tears to grant him the gifts necessary to discharge his duty of Master. "Lord," he cried, "save me, for truth is vanishing from among the children of men." He prayed and wept for a long time; at last he fell asleep. "Friar Thomas, wherefore these prayers, these tears?"—"Because I am being compelled to

[7] Sermon *de Vetula.*

assume the task of teaching and I have not the necessary knowledge. And I do not know what thesis to
argue for my reception."—"Assume the task of
teaching in peace: God is with thee. And for thy
inaugural lecture, expound only these words: 'He
watereth the hills from his chambers: the earth is
satisfied with the truth of thy works.' " [8] The text
of that inaugural dissertation of St. Thomas has
been discovered. He describes therein the grandeur
of the task of teaching doctrine and the method
proper to be followed in imparting wisdom: "God
communicates it by His own particular virtue;
with His own hands He watereth the hills. Teachers,
on the contrary, communicate it only ministerially,
so that the fruit of the hills is to be attributed not to
the hills, but to the works of God."

Friar Thomas taught daily on the Montagne
Sainte Geneviève in the convent of St. Jacques from
one of the two chairs of theology reserved to the
Preachers and incorporated in the University of
Paris. All the religious present in the convent sat
before him on the straw and listened to his lectures
—for none was excused attendance at the theological course—and a great multitude of students from
outside, men soundly disciplined in dialectic, who,
for the most part, had already taught in the Faculty

[8] *Ps.*, ciii, 13.

34

of Arts. On days of solemn disputation, the high dignitaries of the University, the bishop himself, came to witness the contest.

He became famous at once and everybody hastened to his lectures. He had arrived in the heat of the battle, at a time when error was multiple and ubiquitous; he had to grapple with opponents on all sides and in the first place to parry the attack of Guillaume de Saint-Amour and the seculars, who denied the Mendicant Friars the right to teach and described these "false apostles," forever abroad on the highways, these uncommissioned adventurers, as the forerunners of Antichrist. A first debate of the utmost importance was engaged on the liberty of teaching. The very existence of the two new Orders, the Preachers and the Minors, was at stake and there was already manifest the vain pride of that University of Paris which was presently to boast itself the light of the world before dishonouring itself by its condemnation of Joan of Arc. At one moment it appeared as though Rome had been won to the cause of the seculars: it abolished the privileges enjoyed by the religious and then thought better of it. Guillaume de Saint-Amour and the secular Masters, enraged at the sudden reversal, wrote their collective pamphlet *On the dangers of the present time.* Friar Thomas refuted them in his tract *Contra im-*

pugnantes (1257). Guillaume's book was condemned and burned in the court of Rome and himself banished from France by St. Louis.

After three years' theological teaching as Master in Paris (during which he wrote the commentaries upon the *De Trinitate* and the *De Hebdomadibus* of Boethius, the commentaries on *Isaias* and *St. Matthew*, the *Disputed Questions De Veritate*, the first *Quodlibetal Questions* and the greater part of the *Summa Contra Gentiles*), Friar Thomas returned to Italy, in 1259, at the summer holidays (29th June). He remained there for nine years, first in the papal court at Anagni and Orvieto, then at Rome in the convent of Santa Sabina, and again at the Curia at Viterbo. The Popes unceasingly encouraged him. Alexander IV had immediately realized his genius. Urban IV and Clement IV also showed him particular affection. The mission received from the visible head immediately sanctioned with the splendour and precision of an extraordinary privilege of predestination the spirit invisibly received—and the spirit was equal to the task imposed.

Thomas Aquinas performed his work in the spirit of a missionary delegated by the Church and the Church from the very beginning of that work made it her own.

The Master worked incessantly, exhibiting a

formidable power of intellection and a tenacious, unruffled activity (eye-witnesses relate that he not only dictated to three and even four secretaries at once on different subjects, but that there were also times when he lay down to rest in the middle of his dictation and continued dictating in his sleep). He spent himself without counting the cost, well knowing that, while contemplation is above time, action, which takes place in time, must proceed rapidly and defeat by force the malice of the minute; the achievement which dominates the flux of the ages like some huge peaceful pyramid was performed in haste, but betrays no sign of haste, because it overflowed entirely from the fulness of contemplation in a heart united to eternity.

The fundamental work undertaken at the instigation of the Popes, the commentaries upon Aristotle, which were to purge the Philosopher of pagan and Averroist errors and render him suitable for Catholic philosophy to assimilate, were for the most part composed during that sojourn in Italy [9] (commentaries on the *Physics*, the *Metaphysics*, the *nicomachean Ethics*, the *De Sensu et Sensato*, the *De Memoria et Reminiscentia*, the *Second Analytics* and the first four books of the *Politics*). In those years, also, the *Summa contra Gentiles*, the first

[9] According to Grabmann (*Mittelalterliches Geistesleben*, 1926, ch. viii), the commentaries upon the *Physics*, the *Metaphysics*, the *Ethics* and the *Politics* must have been written after the year 1268.

commentary on the epistles of St. Paul, the commentaries on the *Canticle of Canticles*, on *Lamentations*, on *Jeremias*, the *Golden Chain*, the treatise *Of Monarchical Government*, part of the *Disputed Questions* (notably *De Potentia* and *De Malo*) were completed. The *Summa Theologica* was begun.

In November, 1268, Friar Thomas was suddenly sent to Paris where the situation had become serious and Siger de Brabant, a bold and captivating intellect, threatened to secure the triumph of Averroes in the Faculty of Arts under the colours of Aristotle and so to compromise the whole Peripatetic movement. Four more years of strenuous fighting and inconceivable activity followed, years which saw the composition of the treatises *On the Perfection of the Spiritual Life* directed against the enemies of the religious orders, *On the Unity of the Intellect* against the Averroists, *On the Eternity of the World* against the detractors of Aristotle, the commentaries upon the *De Causis*, the *Meteorics*, the *Perihermeneias* and the treatise *De Anima*, upon *Job* and *St. John*, the last *Disputed Questions*, the second part of the *Summa Theologica;* finally, the greater part of the *Quodlibetal Questions* which relate to a method of teaching greatly developed, apparently, and perhaps instituted by St. Thomas himself during his two sojourns in Paris, on the occasion of his dispute with the secular doctors. The

religious, the doctors asserted, were perpetual vaga-
bonds, unfit to become serious, really competent
teachers. Accordingly, in the great disputations
which were held twice yearly, at Christmas and
Easter, and of which the *Quodlibetal Questions* are
the record in writing, Friar Thomas showed that a
religious was capable of answering any question
whatsoever propounded by anyone whomsoever.

After Easter of 1272, he was recalled by his superiors to Italy to establish there a *studium generale*
of theology. He was allowed to choose his own site
and he chose Naples. There he worked upon the
third part of the *Summa Theologica*, composed the
precious *Compendium Theologiae*,[10] commented
the Psalms, the Epistle to the Romans and Aristotle's
treatises on the Sky and the World and on Generation and Corruption.

When he went for a walk in the fields with his
companions, the peasants turned round to gaze in
astonishment at his stature. He was tall and dark,
inclined to corpulence and held himself erect. His
complexion was the colour of wheat, his head big
and rather bold. The Viterbo portrait, more or less
successfully copied and restored, shows a face im-

[10] According to Père Mandonnet's latest investigations (cf. *Revue thomiste,*
1927, p. 157, and the introduction to the latest edition of the *Opuscula*
[Lethielleux]), the *Compendium* was composed in the years 1272–1273. The
Sermons to students are also to be attributed to these years.

pressed with an admirable pacific and unaffected power; the eyes under the high and candid arches of the eyebrows are serene like the eyes of a child; the features are regular and rather heavy with obesity, but consolidated by the force of the intellect behind; the mouth is sensitive with regular, well-defined curves, a mouth which never told a lie. His flesh, according to William of Tocco, was the delicate and sensitive flesh which Aristotle says is peculiar to those endowed with great power of intellect. He was so sensitive that the least bodily hurt gave him exquisite pain. But if he had to be bled (and bleedings were of frequent occurrence in those robust times and even prescribed by the rules of the Order) or cauterized, he had only to meditate and soon fell into such an abstraction of mind that they could do as they liked with him, he felt nothing more. In the refectory, his eyes were perpetually fixed on things above and they could take away and replace his plate again and again without his being aware of it. His *socius*, Reginald of Piperno, was forced to assume the rôle of foster-brother and put before him the dishes he had to eat, removing such as might have done him harm.

The faculty of abstraction, which had developed in him to an extraordinary degree, sometimes played him tricks. Dining once with St. Louis (whose invitation he had been compelled by order of the Prior

40

to accept, because it meant tearing himself away from the *Summa Theologica* which he was dictating at the time), he suddenly brought his fist down on the table and exclaimed: "There is the conclusive argument against the Manichaean heresy!" "Master," said the Prior, "be careful: you are sitting at the moment at the table of the King of France," and plucked him violently by the sleeve to bring him out of his meditation. The king had a secretary quickly summoned and writing materials. Another time, in Italy, a Cardinal asked to see him. Friar Thomas came down from his work, saw nobody and went on meditating; then exclaimed in delight: "Now I've got what I was looking for." He had again to be plucked by the sleeve to take notice of the Lord Cardinal, who, receiving no mark of reverence, had begun to despise him.

He lived in the solitude of his mind, went his way in a density of silence, with only the throb of his prayers and speculations in his ears, following a line which never deviated. Throughout the whole course of his studies and the long years of preparation, he had applied his whole energy to an incredible effort of concentration, accumulating in his prodigious memory all the learning of his masters and his books, leaving nothing that was not penetrated by the mind and transmuted by the mind into life. (And he maintained that intellectual discipline to the end, never leaving a doubt without throwing some light upon it or any true observation from whatever source without storing it away, exercising in a word the utmost vigilance and keeping himself free from everything else.) When at last the time came to speak—*in medio Ecclesiae aperuit os ejus*—he put forth his whole strength to remain invincibly attached to his single ambition: to discern and to demonstrate primary Truth.

Every exterior advantage was, to be sure, but a mere trifle in comparison with the universe in which he lived. (The dialogue between the Master and his students as they returned together from a visit to Saint Denis is familiar: "Master, how beautiful is this city of Paris!" "Yes, indeed, a beautiful city." "If only it belonged to you!" "And what should I do with it?" "You would sell it to the King of France and with the money you would build all the convents the Preaching Friars need." "In truth, I would rather have at this moment the homilies of Chrysostom upon St. Matthew.") But consider the interior use he made of his talents and a genius capable of capsizing the strongest soul; there was a heroic will which, rooted in boundless charity, kept everything within bounds and ensured the absolute rectitude of the moral life amid the violence and diversity of intellectual attractions. All his learning was employed in the service of others. His immense

42

labour was directed not by his own choosing, but by the orders of Providence. He was at the mercy of one after another and they were not backward in overwhelming him with queries and requests for advice; in Paris the King of France took counsel from him, confided in him at evening the difficulties which harassed him and in the morning received the solutions. Herein also Friar Thomas fulfilled his theologian's task, for sacred doctrine is both speculative and practical. And it was his exclusive task. He had only one thing to do and he did it well. He suppressed every more or less parasitical curiosity in which his intelligence might have excelled, whatever hopes it might have offered of magnificent discoveries. The temptation to abandon the intellectual life and to decline into practical activity—a temptation familiar to everyone engaged in the work of the mind, even to a master in theology—was a temptation he never experienced because he drank from a certain secret spring far superior to the intellectual life itself, a spring which made him detached from everything, both from himself and his learning. It was, therefore, in vain that he superabounded in spiritual riches, he was truly poor in spirit. Look for him, Thomas, the son of Landulf and Theodora, where was he to be found? Obliterated, lost in light. A sign so pure that it disappeared before what it pointed out—you looked at him and

43

you saw only what he showed you, that, and the radiance of the face of God.

And he had doubtless received too many graces of illumination, he knew the nature of the creature too well, to be able to consider himself anything in the sight of God. But then what would he have received had he not possessed this very humility? He confessed to his students that he had never experienced a moment's conscious feeling of vainglory. One day, at Bologna, a Friar belonging to another convent, who was unacquainted with him and who had received permission from the Prior to go into the town accompanied by the first Friar he should meet, found him meditating in the cloister: "Good brother, Father Prior says that you are to come with me." Master Thomas Aquinas at once followed that Friar, accompanied him wherever he went and was chided for not walking fast enough, being less disposed to walking than to obedience, "the perfection," as he said, "of every religious life, because therein man subjects himself to his fellow-man for God's sake, as God for man's sake became obedient to man."

His students often marvelled that he, who was so uncompromising in the defence of truth, bore personal attacks so placidly. A lofty magnanimity made him look upon many things as of trifling account. Of lively disposition, he would have inclined naturally to irony, but meekness had conquered irony. He never meddled in other people's business, hated the rash judgment, and had rather appear simple-minded than lightly think evil; the perfection of the speculative intellect moreover suffered no hurt from any error in merely contingent matter. One day a Friar in jovial mood exclaimed: "Friar Thomas, come and see a flying ox!" Friar Thomas came up to the window. The other burst out laughing: "Better believe that an ox can fly," said the Saint, "than think that a religious can tell an untruth."

Tocco and the witnesses at the trial of his canonization have deposed that he was "soft-spoken, easy in conversation, cheerful and bland of countenance; good in soul, generous in conduct; most patient, most prudent; all radiant with charity and gentle piety; wondrous compassionate towards the poor"; filled with love for the Sacrament of the altar, devoted to the Saints, to Our Lady, the apostle Paul and the blessed Dominic. He carried on his person some relics of St. Agnes, which one day cured Reginald of a fever; thereafter he promised to entertain the brethren and students of the Naples convent to a good meal on the Saint's day. He himself was near to death and could fulfil his promise only once.

It was commonly believed, the same witnesses declare, that he had remained as chaste as on the day he left his mother's womb. His whole life was spent in prayer and study, in writing or dictation, in teaching or preaching, so that there was not a moment but was usefully employed. (He preached, either in Latin before the Roman Curia or the University or in Paris, or in his own country in Neapolitan; he never had time to learn any other vulgar tongue. He preached a course of Lenten sermons once at Naples which so powerfully impressed the hearts of his audience that he had to interrupt his discourse to let the congregation weep.) He was ever the first to rise at night for prayer, and as soon as he heard the rest of the brethren coming in answer to the bell, he withdrew into his own room. After his Mass, which he said early in the morning, he heard another Mass for devotion and then mounted the rostrum to deliver his lecture. Thereafter he wrote and dictated. He then took his meal and returned to his cell, where he devoted himself to divine things until the time came to rest. As soon as he awoke, he began again to write. The brethren would fetch him into the garden for recreation, but he would quickly withdraw and return to his room. Whenever he wanted to recreate his body, he walked alone in the cloister, head erect.

He was absolutely simple, utterly ingenuous, devoted to his brethren. He wept for the sins of another as though they had been his own. Such was

46

the purity of his heart, that, according to the testimony of Reginald, his confessor, his general confession before he died was the confession of a child of five.

From the earliest days of his teaching, at the time when he lectured in Paris on the Master of the Sentences, he had risen like a portent in the sky. Some were indignant, the majority marvelled, at such freshness and youth. "A new method, new arguments, new points of doctrine, a new series of problems, a new light," he was a great innovator, because he was not in quest of novelty, but Truth alone; he took the rust off scholasticism.

The novelty *par excellence*, which a few of his predecessors, most notably Albert the Great, had sought to introduce, although its successful achievement was reserved for him, was the integration of Aristotle in Catholic philosophy. Aristotle, who had arrived successively and piecemeal, had for the past half century been making a fearful inroad into Christianity. It was not merely that he brought in his train a crowd of Jews and Arabs whose commentaries were fraught with danger: the noble treasure of natural wisdom which he imported was full of pagan poisons and the mere dazzling glitter of the promises of pure reason was sufficient to bewilder an ingenuous and inquisitive world. The Church, in her prudence, had at first treated the

Philosopher as suspect and allowed only masters to study him in private. Yet every day he made fresh progress. Were the gods of antiquity to triumph over the Christian heart?

Thanks to Thomas Aquinas, the thirteenth century successfully achieved in the sphere of metaphysics and theology what the fifteenth and sixteenth centuries failed to do in the sphere of art and the allurements of the senses. It did not excommunicate Aristotle and the whole effort of reason; it did not yield or apostatize before them; it converted them. St. Thomas transformed, without deforming, Aristotle; not content with restoring his true meaning where the commentators had perverted it, with completing and correcting him wherever he was mistaken or hesitated, he worked the miracle of extricating from the Aristotle of history— "changed by Theology in his very self"—a pure Aristotelian from much more purely Aristotelian than Aristotle himself had ever known. Aristotle was for St. Thomas above all the treasurer of natural reason; with Aristotle it was the whole of antiquity that he adopted, at the same time retaining whatever valuable elements had been imported by Jew and Arab. So also he gathered together every testimony contained in Holy Scripture and the Fathers, the whole of Christian speculation, in such a way that "because he had the utmost reverence for" the Fathers

48

and holy Doctors who had preceded him, "he seems to have inherited the intellect of all." [11] The novelty he introduced was thus a novelty not of destruction but of achievement. His originality consists in having his philosophy taught by everyone. He is not merely the disciple of uncreated Wisdom, of the wisdom of the saints and the wisdom of the philosophers—did he not once allow himself to be instructed at Cologne by an ignorant fellow-pupil?— he is also the disciple of the human race.

The universal inheritance taken up in its entirety and in its entirety reconstructed, born again in the intellect, is quite the opposite of eclecticism and a mosaic of opinions. An immaterial word, infinitely complex in structure and perfectly one in essence, was vitally begotten in the womb of the mind. Nothing could be loftier than such a synthesis, nothing could require greater independence and a more precise personal vigour of thought. But, again, no work is in itself more impersonal. The philosophy of St. Thomas is not the property of St. Thomas. It is the common property of the Church and mankind. It is the only philosophy whose peculiar characteristic is that it is peculiar to nobody, strictly impersonal, absolutely universal. "Common truth," said Giacomo di Viterbo even in his day to Bartolommeo di Capua, "common clarity, common

[11] An observation of Cajetan's adopted by Pope Leo XIII and Pope Pius XI.

enlightenment, common order, and a philosophy which quickly leads to perfect understanding." That is the reason why "it is not Catholicism which is Thomist, but Thomism which is Catholic; and it is Catholic because it is universalist." [12] And the whole of reality is to be found in it unimpaired. If Friar Thomas dwelt in the deep seclusion of his philosophy, the eyes of his reflection were open wide on things—and with what innocent simplicity! He never forces them, never arranges them with artful care, never plays any tricks of light and shade or indulges in exaggerations of relief, tricks which all philosophers, Aristotle excepted, play in secret. He employs his great artistic gifts solely for precision of expression and exactitude of judgment. He knows no compromise with truth: he sets it forth in all its grandeur. Men may say: "A harsh doctrine!" It makes no difference. Such pacific wisdom carries the investigations of reason—absolutely human in philosophy, superelevated by faith in theology— through the whole range of the created and the un-created, but it measures the spirit everywhere against what is, compelling it to respect both the twilight below due to the obscurity of matter, and the night above due to the too lucid transparency of divine things. Fundamentally opposed to agnosti-cism and rationalism, opposite engines which both

[12] H. Woroniecki.

divorce the mind from mystery, Thomist realism weds mind and mystery in the heart of being.

Theology makes use of philosophy and illuminates it by judging it in its own light. So St. Thomas transplanted Aristotelian concepts to a new climate —a supernatural climate—in which faith forces them to produce in our minds some knowledge of the mysteries of God. There is a Thomist philosophy —based upon the sole evidence of reason. St. Thomas achieved a great philosophical work, he had an extraordinary metaphysical genius. But he is not simply, or primarily, a philosopher, he is essentially a theologian. It is as a theologian, from the summit of knowledge which is architectonic *par excellence*, that he definitively establishes the order of Christian economy.

Against the old scholasticism, incapable of recognizing in him the true heir of Augustine, he defends the rights of truth in the natural sphere and the value of reason; against the Averroists, incapable of recognizing in him the true interpreter of Aristotle, he defends the rights of revealed truth and the value of faith. Affirming both the essential naturality of metaphysics and the essential supernaturality of the infused virtues, and the essential subordination of the natural to the supernatural, proclaiming both that grace perfects, without destroying, nature and that the specifically divine life, which grace implants in us, can alone heal the wounds of nature and must take hold of nature absolutely, his peculiar achievement was to bring all the virtues of the mind into the service of Jesus Christ. The whole problem of culture and humanism presented itself in him and his answer was: *sanctity*. Man becomes perfect only supernaturally: he develops only on the cross. A humanism is possible, but on condition that its ultimate end is union with God through the humanity of the Mediator and that it proportions its means to that essentially supernatural end, a humanism of the Incarnation: on condition that it orders itself entirely to love and contemplation; that it entirely subordinates, like the holy soul of Thomas Aquinas itself, mere knowledge to wisdom, and metaphysical wisdom to theological wisdom and theological wisdom to the wisdom of the saints; that it realizes that the form of reason can subject the world only if it is itself subject to the supra-rational and supra-human order of the Holy Ghost and His gifts. Otherwise humanism, even Christian humanism, will inevitably tend to the destruction of man and a universal ruin.

Friar Thomas, Tocco tells us, was a marvellous contemplative, *vir miro modo contemplativus*. If his sanctity was the sanctity of the mind, it was because in him the life of the mind was fortified and transilluminated entirely by the fire of infused contemplation and the gifts of the Holy Ghost. He passed his life in a sort of perpetual rapture and ecstasy. He prayed unceasingly, wept, fasted, yearned. Every syllogism of his is the concretion, as it were, of his prayers and tears. The kind of grace of lucid appeasement which his words procure us derives undoubtedly from the fact that the least of his statements remains invisibly saturated with his yearning and the concentrated passion of the most vehement love. Do not his contemporaries record that, during his lifetime, his mere physical appearance brought a grace of spiritual consolation? The masterpiece of strict and rigorous intellectuality, of intrepid logic, thus overflowed from a heart possessed by charity. On his return to Naples after the death of Thomas, "My Master," Reginald related, "refused to allow me, so long as he lived, to reveal the wonders I saw with my own eyes. It was not so much to the effort of his mind that he was beholden for his learning as to the force of his prayers. Whenever he wanted to study, to debate, to teach, to read or to write, he would first have recourse to the secrecy of prayer, in tears before God to discover in truth the divine secrets, and the result of his prayer was that, whereas before praying he had been in doubt, he came away instructed." When doubtful points occurred to him, it is recorded by Bartolommeo di Capua, he would go to the altar and stand there with much weeping and sobbing, then return to his cell and resume his writing.

"His gift of prayer," writes Tocco, "exceeded all bounds; he raised himself in God as freely as though no burden of flesh had kept him back. Not a day passed but he was ravished out of his senses." He often wept while praying. He never busied himself with temporal affairs, and he had been accustomed from youth upwards abruptly to quit any conversation of which the theme was not the things of God. "No occupation changed the movement of his heart," or diverted him from the prayers in which, once his commerce with men was over, he found himself again unharmed. Very often, during Mass, he burst into tears. Sometimes the congregation witnessed it. Once, as he was saying Mass on Passion Sunday before a crowded congregation of soldiers in the convent at Naples, he appeared in such an ecstasy of spirit and wept so copiously that it seemed as though he were present in person at Calvary and bowed beneath the weight of the sufferings of Christ. Many a time too he wept at Compline, when during Lent they intoned the verse: "Cast me not off in the time of my old age: when my strength shall fail, do not forsake me." At night, after a short sleep, he remained prostrate in prayer in his cell or in the church.

The extraordinary graces with which he was sev-

eral times favoured must be ascribed to the con-
tinuous current of an exalted mystical life. The
Blessed Virgin appeared to him one day to give him
full assurance with regard to his life and doctrine,
and to reveal to him that his state, as he had so often
requested, would never be changed (that is to say
that he would never be raised to any prelacy). Another time it was the Saints who came and helped
him with his commentary upon *Isaias*. An obscure
passage presented a difficulty to him; he had long
been fasting and praying to discover its meaning.
And behold one night Reginald heard him convers-
ing with someone in his room. When the noise of
conversation ceased, Friar Thomas called him, bade
him light the candle and take the manuscript of the
commentary on *Isaias*. He dictated for an hour,
then sent him back to bed. But Reginald fell upon
his knees: "I will not rise from here until you tell
me the name of him or them with whom you con-
versed so long this night." Friar Thomas at the last
began to weep and, forbidding him in God's name to
make the matter public during his life, confessed
that the apostles Peter and Paul had come to instruct
him. Once there was revealed to him a temptation
which obsessed a brother, twice he had a vision of
the soul of his sister Marotta, a Benedictine abbess,
who first asked him for Masses to deliver her from
Purgatory, then told him of her deliverance and

acquainted him that Rainaldo, who had been unjustly put to death by Frederick II, was in Heaven; an angel then showed him a book inscribed in letters of azure and gold, where his brother's name was written in the golden pages devoted to the martyrs, because he had been executed for fidelity to the Pope. Another day there appeared to him a friend of his, a master in theology, one Friar Romano, who had lately died, and the apparition discussed with him questions they had debated on earth. At Paris, when the Masters sought his advice as to the proper method of teaching the mystery of the Eucharist, he went first and laid his answer on the altar, imploring the crucifix; brethren who were watching him suddenly saw Christ standing in front of him on the draft which he had written and heard these words: "Thou hast written well concerning this Sacrament of My Body and thou hast well and truthfully resolved the problem which had been put to thee, so far as it is possible to be known on earth and described in human words." And the force of ecstasy was such that the Saint rose a cubit in the air. A similar incident occurred again at Naples. Friar Thomas was then writing the third part of the *Summa* dealing with the Passion and Resurrection of Christ. One day, before Matins, the sacristan saw him raised nearly two cubits above the ground and stood a long time gazing at him. Suddenly he heard a voice proceed from the image on the crucifix to which the Doctor was turned, praying in tears: "Thou hast written well of me, Thomas. What reward shall I give thee for thy work?"—"None but Thyself, O Lord!"

We have information therefore regarding the mystical life of St. Thomas in the testimonies of his brethren and exterior indications. Many a personal note in his writings is equally revelatory, while his own teaching on the nature of infused wisdom also bewrays, in his own despite, his experience of divine things; lastly, his work is the proof *par excellence* of the superhuman illuminations in the midst of which it was produced. There is, however, never a direct statement by himself, for he practised only too thoroughly the maxim of St. Anthony the hermit which he may have read in Cassian (every day he had read to him a few pages of Cassian), that "there can be no perfect prayer, if the religious perceives himself to be praying." And it was no part of his mission, like a St. John of the Cross or a St. Teresa, to expound the things of contemplation practically, from the point of view of introspection and experience. The secret of that mystical life, of which all we know from extrinsic indications is that it was one of the most exalted conceivable, is therefore well preserved. All we are entitled to presume is that the duty of teaching imposed for the benefit of the Church and the world must have drawn into a particularly luminous sphere the secret universe of the contemplative gifts, and there substituted, perhaps, for the customary passive purifications the kind of uninterrupted passion suffered by the mind when it is rivetted to its mission, and must have blended the obscurity of negative theology and the wisdom of love in which the heart of the Master dissolved for sweetness with the clarity of the charismata of prophecy (the penetration of divine things) and the manifestation of wisdom (*sermo sapientiae*).

The prayers composed by St. Thomas are not confessions but compositions again proceeding from his profound life, and, for all their beauty, they give no indication of the nature of that life; they are compositions as limpid as the sky, and always, with sublime simplicity, declare their purpose. There is no purer poem than, none containing so much devotion in so much light as, the Office of the Blessed Sacrament. It was surely in obedience to some design of providential harmony that Pope Urban in 1264, nine years after the death of the Blessed Julienne du Mont-Cornillon,[13] invited the Saint to compose the office of the new feast which the Lord had been asking for the past thirty years.

---

[13] Dom Baudot (*Dict. d'Hagiographie*, p. 387), states that Julienne du Mont-Cornillon died on the 5th April, 1255.

In the doctrine, as in the Sacrament, it is the same truth which incorporates within itself the unity of the Church. As Thomas Aquinas had received the mission to teach the doctrine, so he was instructed also to hymn the Sacrament.

Could any ordeal be more severe for such a Master than to feel that his teaching was suspect in the Church? The four years of heroic struggle which occupied his last sojourn in Paris were darkened by the shadow of such an ordeal.

Averroist philosophers who idolized Aristotle, self-styled Augustinian theologians who were afraid of the mind, a short-sighted crowd rose up against him and strove to rend the seamless garment of his too pure doctrine. Against the former he was forced to attack Aristotle whom Averroes had "corrupted": against the latter he was forced to defend the genuine Aristotle. And, doubtless, even in Paris, he had numerous fervent disciples, in the Faculty of Arts especially, which had not been wholly conquered by Siger de Brabant and Boethius of Dacia; they greeted his lectures on Aristotle with enthusiasm and after his death implored the Dominicans to give them his body and his writings. No doubt he had the authority of the Pope on his side and the curia, whose theologian he was; he could always, in case of need, appeal to the Roman Church. But nearly all the masters in theology of the University opposed him, seculars and Franciscans (for such quarrels even then were vigorous) wanted to be rid of him and the Bishop of Paris supported them. And it was because the interests of the Faith were at stake, they said, that they would have felled him.

His great controversy with Siger took place in 1270, on the occasion of the publication of the latter's *De Anima Intellectiva*. Thomas retorted with his *De Unitate Intellectus*.[14] That same year also he was compelled to meet the criticisms of his other opponents, the pseudo-Augustinians of the Faculty of Theology, against whom he composed his *De Aeternitate Mundi*. In a solemn disputation held towards the approach of Easter on the thesis of his doctrine which they most bitterly opposed (the theory of the intellective soul as the unique substantial form in man), Friar John Peckham, regent of the Friars Minor, attacked him in a bombastic and violent harangue;[15] his own brethren abandoned him, some even argued against him, the bishop and the doctors awaited his downfall and

[14] Such, at any rate, is the opinion expressed by Père Mandonnet in his book on *Siger de Brabant*. Père Chossat, however, considers (*Revue de Philosophie*, 1914, vols. xxiv and xxv) that Siger's *De Anima Intellectiva* is itself an answer to the *De Unitate Intellectus* of St. Thomas, which was written to refute another work by Siger, *Super III⁰ de Anima*.

[15] [Even so, we should be grateful to John Peckham, Archbishop of Canterbury, for the beautiful sequence *Meditatio in Festo Corporis Christi*, which one of the most accomplished humanists of his time, the late Professor J. S. Phillimore, had no hesitation in including among *The Hundred Best Latin Hymns* (Gowans & Gray, Ltd., London, 1926).]

did all they could to procure it. But his words passed peacefully through their midst and every attempt failed against his mildness. The bishop of Paris, Étienne Tempier, who would have included the thesis in question (along with another of Thomas Aquinas on the simplicity of spiritual substances) in the condemnation he was preparing of some of Siger's propositions, was forced to abandon his project and to condemn only the Averroist propositions (10th December, 1270). But on the 7th March, 1277, three years day for day after the death of the Doctor, in renewing his condemnation of Averroism he tacked on to the theses of Siger de Brabant and Boethius of Dacia which he censured some twenty Thomist propositions. Some days later, on the 18th March, 1277, the Dominican Robert Kilwardby, Archbishop of Canterbury and Primate of England, also condemned the philosophy of Thomas Aquinas, more particularly the famous thesis of the unicity of the substantial form in man, which at the time caused "almost infinite scandal" in the schools of England. In 1284 the Archbishop was succeeded by John Peckham who increased the gravity of the censure. Room had to be found for Duns Scotus and the nominalist debaters who were to darken counsel in the fourteenth century! The Middle Ages in their decline refused to listen to the voice of Rome and failed to use the gift of God.

Friar Thomas returned to Italy after Easter in 1272, took part in the Chapter-General of his Order held in Florence and then went on to Naples to continue his teaching. One day, the 6th December, 1273, as he was celebrating Mass in the chapel of St. Nicholas, a great change came over him. From that moment onward he ceased to write or dictate.[16] Was the *Summa* then, with its thirty-eight treatises, its three thousand articles and ten thousand objections, to remain unfinished? Reginald ventured to complain: "I can do no more," said his master. Reginald insisted: "Reginald, I can do no more; such things have been revealed to me that everything I have written seems to me rubbish. Now, after the end of my work, I must await the end of my life."

The finger of God was dissevering the soul from the body. A few days later he expressed the desire to see his sister, the Countess di Sanseverino, whom he tenderly loved, and he made a great effort at the cost of much fatigue to pay her a visit. But as he drew nigh, and she came forth to meet him, he scarcely addressed her a word. She was alarmed and accosted

---

[16] The divine influence had been too profound for it to be possible for him to devote himself thenceforward to his ordinary work. He made a violent effort, however, while on his way to the Council of Lyons, and composed his short *Responsio ad Bernardum Abbatem*; and on his death-bed he composed for the monks of Fossanova his second commentary (now lost) on the *Canticle of Canticles*: his second *commentary*, not his third; for of the other two commentaries attributed to St. Thomas only one is genuine.

Reginald: "What ails my brother? He looks dazed and answers me not a word." "He has been in that state since the feast of St. Nicholas," answered Reginald, "and has ceased to write."

In January, Gregory X summoned him to the Council which he had convoked at Lyons. Thomas set out with Reginald. They journeyed together on mules. Reginald hazarded a few words in an attempt to distract him: "You and Friar Bonaventura will be created Cardinals to the great glory of your Orders."—"I shall never be anything in our Order or in the Church," replied Friar Thomas. "I cannot serve our Order better in any other state than my present one."

He stopped on the way at the castle of his niece, the Countess Francesca, at Maenza in Campania. He had scarcely arrived when he fainted for weariness, and sickness took hold of him. Then Providence made him a present of a little fish. He had lost his appetite and felt no inclination for anything but the fresh herring he had eaten in France. Reginald was heartbroken, for that northern specialty was not to be found in Italy. But they opened a basket of a merchant passing with a load of sardines and found it miraculously full of fresh herring which everyone in the castle ate.

Thomas remained only four days at Maenza. Feeling seriously ill, he asked with great devotion that they would transport him to the neighbouring monastery of Santa Maria at Fossanova. As he made his way in, he leaned against the wall and said: "This is my rest for ever and ever: here will I dwell, for I have chosen it." [17] It was a Cistercian Monastery; he had returned to St. Benedict to die. He lay ill for a month in great patience and humility. The monks carried in faggots from the forest with their own hands to make him a fire, considering it unseemly that beasts of burden should bear a load of wood for the use of so distinguished a man, and as often as he saw them enter his bedroom, he would raise himself humbly and with great respect, saying: "How comes it that holy men bring me wood?" At the prayer of some of the monks, he shortly commented upon the *Canticle of Canticles*; he then asked for the viaticum. The Abbot, surrounded by his monks, brought him the Body of Our Lord. When he saw the Host, he threw himself upon the ground, burst into tears and greeted It with words of wonderful and prolonged adoration: "I receive Thee, Price of my redemption, Viaticum of my pilgrimage, for love of Whom I have studied and kept vigil, toiled, preached and taught. Never have I said aught against Thee; if I have done so, it was through ignorance and I do

[17] *Ps.,* cxxxi, 14.

not persist in my intention, and if I have done anything ill, I leave the whole to the correction of the
Roman Church. In that obedience I depart from
this life." He died three days later, on the 7th
March, 1274, in the forty-ninth year of his age.

The Sub-Prior of the monastery, whose eyes were
far gone, recovered his sight on pressing his face
against the face of the Saint. A multitude of other
miracles followed; and many were nevertheless concealed by the monks, according to the evidence of
Bartolommeo di Capua, for fear that the holy
body might be taken away from them. They
exhumed it seven months later to find it intact and
exhaling such fragant odours that you would have
thought yourself in a laboratory full of sweet-
smelling herbs and the whole monastery was per-
fumed therewith. A second exhumation took place
fourteen years later and the same thing happened.

It is related that Master Albert at Ratisbon,
where he was bishop, knew by revelation that his
great disciple was dead. He wept bitterly at the
time, and ever afterwards when he heard his name
mentioned, he wept again, saying: "He was the
flower and glory of the world." When the rumour
spread that the writings of Friar Thomas were being attacked in Paris, the old Master made the
journey to defend them. On his return, he convoked

a solemn assembly in which he declared that after the work accomplished by Thomas, others would labour in vain.

The antagonism of the theologians, however, in Paris and Oxford was not disarmed; or that of the Franciscan doctors: in 1282 a Chapter-General of Friars Minor, held at Strasburg, prohibited the reading of the *Summa* in Franciscan schools. But "everyone hath his proper gift from God," says St. Paul; and not every Order has the task of teaching theology. The Dominicans, however, had quickly realized that in granting them Thomas Aquinas, God had revealed to them the purpose of their existence. In 1278, at their Chapter-General held in Milan, they had decided to defend his philosophy energetically; it soon became the official teaching of the Order and Pope Clement VI in 1346 bade them never to depart from it. But it is for the common good of the Church and the world that they are charged to maintain that philosophy in its integrity. It is the common patrimony of us all. From the very beginning it was the universal Church, in the person of the Pope, which recognized Thomas for its Doctor: it is the papacy, which discerning in him the common spirit of all tradition, both human and divine, the greatest and most assiduous force of preservation of everything in the past which is superior to time—but also the movement

of life and the most active power of assimilating
and safeguarding everything in the future which
is worth more than the moment—foreseeing the
descent of night, which divides, and resolving to
oppose thereto the great assembly in the mind of
all the things of creation under the accorded light
of reason and faith, sided with Thomas Aquinas
against the routine narrow-mindedness of the
schools and a hidebound conservatism destined
immediately to fall into dissolution. But such sec-
tarian particularisms offered strong resistance. It
took fifty years of violent controversy to put an
end to the calumnies levelled against the orthodoxy
of Thomism. The canonization of Thomas, whose
sanctity was proclaimed by Jean XXII on the 18th
July, 1323, at Avignon, was the last act of the
battle. "Thomas alone has illuminated the Church
more than all the other doctors together," the Pope
declared. "His philosophy can have proceeded only
from some miraculous action of God." That philosophy was thenceforth free to shed its radiance
without hindrance, and on the 14th February,
1324, at the instance of Rome, Étienne de Borreto,
bishop of Paris, withdrew the condemnation of the
Thomist theses decreed in 1277 by his predecessor
Étienne Tempier. Yet, though the glory of Thomas
Aquinas was immense, the already failing Christian
world had not the courage to ask him to cure it

and scholasticism proceeded to squander its strength in futile rivalries and decadent systems.

A new era, however, has dawned for St. Thomas. The Church has recourse to him henceforward in her battle against all the heresies and errors; his philosophy grows greater in the sky, the Church of Christ makes use of it in her own peculiar life, which is one and universal: the Popes bear it testimonies innumerable, the concordance and reiteration of which in the course of centuries are singularly significant. And now Leo XIII in the Encyclical *Aeterni Patris* (4th August, 1879) and Pius X, Benedict XV and Pius XI, in decrees unceasingly renewed, and clearly without imposing that philosophy as an article of faith (no theological or philosophical system could ever be so imposed), have ordered Catholic teachers to make it the basis of their teaching, and implore the world with tragic insistence to return to it for the salvation of the mind and civilization.

He who was deservedly called the Angelic Doctor and the Doctor of the Eucharist is also and in the first place the Common Doctor of the Church, because he alone perfectly answers the universal amplitude of Catholic thought. It is very remarkable that even in Byzantine theology, towards the decline of the Middle Ages, he enjoyed a great reputation.

Summaries and Greek translations of his principal works, the two *Summae*, the Commentaries upon the *De Anima* and the *Physics* of Aristotle, and many *opuscula*, were composed about that time, notably by Demetrios Kydones, the minister of the Emperor John VI Cantacuzene, the translator of the *Summa contra Gentiles* and the adversary of Kabasilas, and by George Scholarios Gennadios, Patriarch of Constantinople. He would now teach the grandeur of God in Arabic and Chinese and Sanscrit, as in Latin and Greek and Russian. He is the true apostle of modern times; his principles are exalted enough and bound together with sufficient strength to embrace in a superior and veracious, not eclectic, unity—a unity of discrimination, order and redemption, not of confusion and death—the immense diversities of race, culture and spirituality which divide the world from east to west. The substance which he brings to men in the Latin order of his exposition transcends every particularity of time and place; he alone can give them back the divine blessing of unity of mind in the only place where it is possible to attain it, the light of the incarnate Word.

II

THE WISE ARCHITECT

Sicut enim novae domus architecto de universa structura curandum est.

II MACHAB., II, 30.

Secundum gratiam Dei, quae data est mihi, ut sapiens architectus fundamentum posui.

I COR., III, 10.

LEIBNIZ already in his day lamented the lost unity of Christian culture, a unity which has been in process of dissolution for the past four centuries.

It has often been observed that in three great spiritual crises, the humanist Renaissance, the Protestant Reformation, and the rationalist *Aufklärung,* man achieved a historical revolution of absolutely unparalleled importance, at the end of which he conceived himself as the centre of his history and the ultimate end of his activity on earth, and arrogated to himself the peculiarly divine privilege of absolute independence or all-sufficiency which theologians term *aseitas.* The immense deployment of brute force over the surface of the globe and the industrial enslavement of matter to which Europe gave itself up in the nineteenth century are merely the expression in the ·sensible

70

order of that spiritual usurpation. A sort of fictitious unity of the human spirit then arose like a great mirage under the optimistic trappings of positivist pseudo-science, and men believed that they were in sight of the goal, that they were about to become masters and owners of themselves, of all nature and history: it was catastrophe which was imminent, and while matter, apparently vanquished and subdued, imposed its rhythm and the endlessly multiplied exigencies of such satisfactions as it procures upon human life, men found themselves more divided than ever, in disunion with other men, in disunion with themselves; matter is a principle of disunion and can only beget division. Nation against nation, class against class, passion against passion, it is human personality in the end which dissolves, and man tries in vain to find himself in the dissociated fragments of his unconscious velleities and inconsistent sincerities—and yet God knows to what diligent scrutiny each is subjected! —while a sort of fever of despair takes hold of the world.

What are the conditions on which this lost unity can be recovered, not as it once was, for time is irreversible, but reconstituted once more in new forms? One truth seems to me to dominate the whole discussion. Man cannot find his unity in himself; he finds it outside himself, above himself.

It was his determination to be self-sufficient which ruined him. He will find himself again only by becoming attached to his first principle and to the order transcending it. Pure subjectivity, like pure materiality, disperses. It was because their attention was fixed upon being and God with an objectivity at once ingenuous and pious, an objectivity transported with love, that the Christian ages had such a clear and precise appreciation of human and moral things—and unity no less. There is no greater delusion than to seek in immanentism the reconciliation of man with himself. Man becomes reconciled with himself only on the cross, which is hard and exterior to him: the cross upon which he is nailed. Objectivity is the first condition of unity.

There are, to be sure, other conditions in the material order and they must not be neglected. But objectivity is primordial because it affects the two activities most worthy of man—the activity of the mind, so far as it is faithful to the object and therefore to the first Being, and the activity of love, so far as it unites us to the principle of our being and our veritable Whole.

The resurrection of metaphysics and a fresh expansion of charity are the essential presuppositions of a return to human unity—to that unity which was perfect only in the Garden of Eden and in

THE WISE ARCHITECT

Gethsemane in the heart of Christ, the longing for which will never cease to haunt us.

If we cut sections, so to speak, in the tissue of human events, we shall find two very different elements at the various moments of history, especially at moments of major transformation; on the one hand, an element of great importance in matter and volume, which represents the massive result, the residue, as it were, of past effort, an element which may be described as the static factor or the resistance factor, signifying above all something done, concluded, finished.

The other element is nothing as regards volume and appearance, but is ever so much more important as regards energy, an element which may be described as the dynamic factor or the factor of living force signifying above all something in the making or about to be made, something in active preparation, with the formal part to play in the generation of the future.

As far as the former element, the static factor, is concerned, what strikes us in the contemporary world, in the world ravaged by capitalism and positivism, in the world dominated by an anti-theological and anti-metaphysical civilization, is that pitiful product which goes by the name of the modern man, a being cut off from all his ontological roots and transcendental objects, who, because he sought to find his centre in himself, has become, in Hermann Hesse's phrase, merely a wolf howling in despair towards eternity. But that very fact also shows us that the world has made and finished with the experiment of positivism, pseudo-scientific scepticism, subjectivist idealism, and that the experiment has been sufficiently demonstrative. Such things are dead: though they may still encumber us for a long time, like cadaverous products, they are finished.

If we consider the other historical element, the dynamic factor in the present-day world, what we perceive on the contrary is a profound, an immense need of metaphysics, a great impulse towards metaphysics, towards the restoration of ontological values. The world which is struggling to be, struggling to emerge in the future, is not a world of positivism but a world of metaphysics.

It is not, alas, sufficient to say: the resurrection of metaphysics. The metaphysics in question must be a real metaphysics. I do not overlook all the services which the Bergsonian movement may, as a matter of fact, have rendered in France, the neo-Hegelian and pluralist movements in England, the phenomenologist movement in Germany. But it must nevertheless be admitted that a metaphysics whose conclusion

74

is pure change and a more or less monist evolution-
ism, or a polytheist moralism or an atheistic ontology,
would be no remedy for humanity. The resurrection
of metaphysics means in the first place that we are
on the threshold of an age of great metaphysical
conflicts, great battles of the spirit; and the com-
batants will not be systems evolved by European
speculation only, but Asiatic systems also rejuve-
nated by modern thinkers of great acumen and distinction, such as are already to be found in Japan
and India.

What guide can we appeal to to lead us through
the maze of all these metaphysical conflicts? Thomas
Aquinas teaches us to distinguish in the intellectual
sphere between good and evil, truth and falsehood,
a process of angelic sifting, as it were; teaches us
how to preserve every true intention contained in
the diversity of systems and to correct the rest in a
synthesis poised upon reality. For one of the peculiar
characteristics of his philosophy, as has often been
observed, is that, so far from being a flabby eclecticism devoid of principles, it is on the contrary a system with principles so exalted and rigid that it
reconciles at its elevation, by transcending them, the
most antinomous theories, which then appear to be
merely the opposite inclines to one same altitude.

St. Thomas, by probing deeply into the intimate
nature of knowledge and the peculiar life of the

mind, founds upon reason more securely than any other philosopher—as against positivism but yet making the fullest allowance for experience and as against idealism but yet making the fullest allowance for the immanent and constructive activity of the spirit—the objectivity of knowledge, the rights and value of the science of being. But also, as against the false metaphysical systems that threaten to assail us, as against the pantheist immanentism which some philosophers would impose upon us in the name of the East, as against the pragmatism of the Far West, as against the atheist intellectualism apparent in Europe, he establishes the transcendence of Him Whom we know through His creatures, but Who has no common standard of comparison with them; Who is Being, Intelligence, Goodness, Life and Beatitude, but Who surpasses and transcends infinitely our ideas of being, goodness, and all the other perfections; Whose nature, in short, our concepts grasp by analogy but are powerless to comprehend.

Metaphysics, therefore, in his hands rises above agnosticism and rationalism; it starts out from experience on its ascent to the uncreated Being and restores in the human spirit the proper hierarchy of the speculative values, inaugurates in us the order of wisdom.

If it be a question thereafter of ethical values and the conduct of human life, then it is only too easy to see to what an extent the modern world is the world of selfishness, meanness and insensibility. Once man undertook to be self-sufficient, what was there to prevent everything in him becoming dissociated and desiccated in irremediable antagonisms? Such at any rate appears to be the case as regards the residue of the near past. And, in truth, love lives only by God and by what it deifies, and when it perceives that what it has deified is but a mere fragment of nothing it turns to contempt and hatred. For this reason the love of humanity without God could not end otherwise than in a state in which the last resource of everyone is merely self-worship or suicide.

As far as the second historical element, the dynamic element above referred to, is concerned, what the contemporary world reveals to us precisely by reason of the kind of impossibility to live which anthropocentric egotism creates, is the need and presentiment of a vast effusion of love. Here again we must be on our guard against counterfeits; as we must be on our guard against false systems of metaphysics, so we must also be on our guard against the delusive forms of love.

A false humanitarian mysticism, pseudo-buddhist, theosophical or anthroposophical, a false reign of the heart which claimed to instal itself at the expense of the mind, in contempt of the Word which creates and forms Its laws, a sort of quietist heresy which reduced us to a condition below the level of man, because we should then have lost the very idea of truth, and dissolved us in an equivocal poetic sensuality, unworthy of the name of truth, are a few of the evils which threaten us from that point of view. We are far removed from the materialism of the nineteenth century: it is from a pseudo-spiritualism and a pseudo-mysticism that we may expect the greatest dangers of deviation in our time.

The Angelic Doctor shows us the direct road, reminds us that order dwells in the heart of holy love, and that if in God subsisting Love proceeds from the Father and the increated Word, love in our case also must proceed from truth and pass through the lake of the Word; otherwise its diffusion only means destruction.

He reminds us also that there is only one effective and authentic way of loving our brethren and that is to love them with that same charity which makes us first love God above all. Thus—according to the admirable order of charity described in the second part of the *Summa*, which embraces all men without injuring the native privileges of any—love which unites us, above being, to the principle of being, descends again upon the creature with a divine force, shatters every obstacle and rekindles every coldness, opens up a new world which reveals the divine attributes in a more profound, unsuspected way, a world in which beings not only know one another but also recognize one another, and makes us wish well to our enemies. So we must assert against the deliquescences of sentimentality and the naturalist worship of the human race the true nature of the divine love.

And against the hardening due to the worship of force, the naturalist worship of the individual, the class, the race or the nation, it is the primacy of that same love which must be asserted. *Caritas major omnium.* Need it be observed that the whole ethical theory of St. Thomas is based upon that doctrine which he derives from the Gospel and St. Paul? He has erected upon that teaching of the Gospel an infrangible theological synthesis, in which he shows how Love, which makes us undeviatingly desire our last end, enjoys an absolute practical primacy over the whole of our individual and social life and constitutes the very bond of perfection, how it is better for us to love God than to know Him, and how no virtue, lacking such love, is truly virtuous or attains its perfect form, not even justice. And St. Thomas knows that such love really dominates human life,

is effective love of God above all things and of one's
neighbour as of one's self, only if it is supernatural,
rooted in faith, proceeding from the grace of Christ,
which makes us, in the image of the Crucified, sons
and heirs of the God Who is Love. If we follow the
Angelic Doctor, we shall realize that peace in man
and among men (the direct work of charity, *opus
charitatis*, "for love is a unifying force and the
efficient cause of unity") descends from that super-
essential Peace and from that eternal Love which
resides in the heart of the Trinity.

The distress of modern times, it was observed in
the beginning of this essay, derives from the fact
that culture, which is a certain perfection of man,
has come to consider itself an ultimate end. It began
by despising in its Cartesian or philosophical phase
everything above the level of reason; it ends by despising reason itself, suffers both the law of the flesh
and the spiritual vertigo which irrationality inevitably precipitates in the case of man. "The error of
the modern world consists in its claim to ensure the
dominance of reason over nature while refusing the
dominance of supernature over reason." [1] This is
the reason why, even in the order of knowledge, the
metaphysics referred to a moment ago remains an
inadequate remedy. Another wisdom, more exalted

[1] Cf. *The Things that are not Caesar's* (Sheed & Ward), p. xxv.

and more divine, is born of love itself, through the gifts of the Holy Ghost. And it is for that mystical wisdom in the first place that our misery hungers and thirsts, because it alone is capable of satisfying our hunger and our thirst, being union in experience with divine things and a beginning of beatitude. And yet it still leaves us hungry and thirsty, because vision alone can fully satiate our desire with God.

St. John of the Cross is the great experimental doctor of such wisdom; St. Thomas Aquinas is its great theologian. And because he has defined more accurately than any other doctor the central truth which cannot be disregarded without dealing a mortal blow to contemplation, and Christianity itself—I mean the distinction between nature and grace, and their active compenetration, and the whole organism of the infused gifts—he provides a better explanation than any other of the true nature of mystical wisdom, and defends it better than any other against every counterfeit.

That is the greatest benefit we may expect from him from the point of view of the restoration of Christian culture; for, in the last resort, it is from that wisdom and contemplation that the whole Christian order on this earth depends.

The unity of a culture is determined in the first place and above all by a certain common philosophical structure, a certain metaphysical and moral attitude, a certain common scale of values, in a word, a certain common conception of the universe, of man and human life, of which social, linguistic, and juridical structures are, so to speak, the embodiment.

This metaphysical unity has long been broken— not certainly completely destroyed, but broken and as it were obliterated in the West. The drama of Western culture consists in the fact that its stock of common metaphysics has been reduced to an utterly inadequate minimum, so that only matter now holds it together, and matter is incapable of keeping anything together. The drama is all the more tragic for us because everything at the moment has to be re-created, everything to be put in place again in our European house. If a common philosophy succeeded in securing acceptance by an élite in Europe, it would be the beginning of the cure of the Western world.

As Thomas Aquinas united in his marvellously tempered constitution the talents of the men of the North and South, of Norman and Lombard, as he integrated in his doctor's mission the Italy of the Popes, the Germany of Albert the Great, the France of St. Louis and the University of Paris, as he combined the treasures of the Greeks and the Latins, the Arabs and the Jews, with the inheritance bequeathed by the Fathers and Christian wisdom, in a word the entire contribution of the known world of his time, so his marvellously synthetic and organic theology, open to every aspect of reality, offers the intellectual tendencies peculiar to the various nations, and more particularly to the three just mentioned, the means of exercising themselves freely, not in mutual destruction, but in mutual completion and consolidation.

The reason is that St. Thomas succeeded in constructing a philosophical and theological wisdom so elevated in immateriality that it is really free of every particularization of race or environment. Alas! what we have witnessed during the past few centuries is an absolutely opposite phenomenon, a kind of racial materialization of philosophy. Descartes is one of the glories of France, but he hypostasizes certain defects, certain temptations peculiar to the French intellectual temperament. Hegel does the same for Germany; William James, the pragmatists and the pluralists, for the Anglo-Saxon countries. It is time to turn to truth itself, which belongs to no particular country, time to turn to the universality of human reason and supernatural wisdom. The necessity is all the more urgent because it appears as though the advent of a new era in philosophy were imminent.

Imagine for a moment that Catholics in the various countries realized the primordial importance of intellectual questions, of metaphysics and theology, that they discarded senseless prejudices against scholasticism, that they considered it, not as a mediæval mummy to be examined with archæological curiosity, but as a living armour of the mind and the indispensable equipment for the boldest enterprises of discovery; imagine that they fulfilled in practice the ardent aspiration of the Church, which is not to conquer adherents as though Catholicism were a human undertaking, but to serve divine Truth everywhere in the souls of men and the universe; imagine that they transcended intestine divisions and the petty rivalries of schools which everywhere sterilize their activity, finally, that they became conscious of the necessity of a serious and sustained intellectual co-operation among Catholics of all nations.

The common Doctor of the Church would then become in all truth their common master; with him to lead them, they might work effectively for the restoration of the West and its unity. Then there would be workers for the harvest. Then in the speculative sphere, Thomist metaphysics might assimilate into a true intellectual order the immense body of the individual sciences, abandoned at the moment to chaos and in danger of having their admirable progress exploited by aberrant philosophies.

In the moral sphere, Thomist metaphysics and theology might architectonically preside over the elaboration of the new social order, the Christian economy, the Christian politics which the present state of the world so urgently requires. Finally, to revert to the great primitive symptoms and the great primitive causes of the divisions afflicting us, humanism, Protestantism, rationalism, at the end of their tether, having had time to suffer to the extreme the process of self-destruction developed by their initial error, and to experience also the value of many a reality which that error fails to take into account, would be astonished to find in the treasury of the Angelic Doctor the very truths which they coveted with no clear perception of their nature and which they have only been able to ruin.

I would add that Greek and Russian piety, which differs apparently from Catholic piety not so much in divergences of dogma as in certain characteristics of spirituality, is much less hostile, in my opinion, to the philosophy of St. Thomas than might at first be supposed. It approaches the problems from another angle and the scholastic presentation as a rule irritates and offends it. These are merely questions of modality; and I am convinced that a proper understanding of the Thomist system would dispel innumerable misunderstandings and facilitate many unexpected encounters. I am also convinced that when our separated brethren are driven, under pressure of contemporary errors, to a more systematic and developed theological defence, they will be constrained to seek in the principles elaborated by St. Thomas trusty weapons against vain philosophy.

In all this St. Thomas appears to us as the great intellectual renovator of the West.

Need it be added that it would argue a very imperfect acquaintance with human nature to believe in the possibility of such a Utopia? Nevertheless, if a serious effort is not made in such a direction, one may as well proclaim that culture in the West is doomed. It may be hoped, in spite of everything, that such an effort will be made.

I have mentioned the West. Where, in point of fact, does the West begin? We should be careful not to form any too restricted idea of it and remember that we are always east of somebody.

The West begins at Golgotha. It is Calvary, the centre of the world, which marks the dividing line between East and West, and there Christ extends His redeeming arms over East and West alike. If we want to form an adequate cultural idea of the Western world, let us say that it is a world whose axis stretches from Jerusalem to Athens and Rome, and from the deserts of Egypt and the Berber lands to the shores of the Atlantic and the northern seas, embracing in one same community the richest variety of national traditions, institutions and cultures.

The Greek and Byzantine culture, oriental in relation to the Latin civilization, the succession of the Western Empire such as history has defined it in the most restricted meaning of the word, is nevertheless an integral part of Western culture. The result of the breach between Constantinople and Rome was to confine it within itself (and yet not so completely as is commonly thought) in the heart of that culture, not to detach it from it entirely.

And if Eurasians are right in considering Russia as a sort of continent by itself in which Europe and Asia are indistinguishable, if the Revolution at the present day drags that continent to the side of Asia, nevertheless, by its cultural past it belongs to the spiritual community of the West.

And now I put the question: Is one entitled on any ground whatsoever to identify the Western world with the Christian religion? No! It would be a deadly and supremely impertinent error, which the tone adopted by certain careless apologists would seem occasionally to commit, but which is essentially repugnant to the characteristic *par excellence*, to the *catholicity*, of the religion of Christ.

Further to suggest that the West has not a particular mission to fulfil in regard to that religion would be another error. Pope Leo XIII himself defined the importance of that mission. If the West, which owes so much to the Church, has done duty so long as the profane embodiment of Christian culture, it is precisely because it was chosen to evangelize the rest of the world—not to enslave the universe to its military or commercial interests, but to serve the universe by bringing to it the message of redemption.

Whatever may have been and whatever may still be the heroic effort of its saints, its missionaries and its martyrs, Western civilization has too long failed to discharge its duty. That duty is now imposed upon it under pain of death: it can now save itself only by working for the whole universe.

To be devoted to the particularities of a country, to its language, customs and liberties and so to continue for a little while longer the beauty of perishable things, the "works and days" stored in the *genius loci,* is the business of poets.[2] The statesman too is, in a way, particularist; for the statesman is concerned with the common good of the country, which must be his first object, but yet in such a way that while loving his own country above all

[2] I do not thereby mean that regional and linguistic particularism does not correspond to conditions which politics is in duty bound to take into account. What I do mean is that no such particularism should be allowed to constitute a political *end* or to circumscribe the peculiar object of politics.

others, he does not therefore cease to admire other countries and to wish them well nor does he injure the rights of the human individual or the interests of the human race.

But in the order of the mind, of speculation, of culture, one must be determinedly universalist. The barriers of intellectual protectionism are now and forever things of the past. Every book, every newspaper article—Catholic writers ought to realize it—finds readers on the banks of the Ganges and the Yellow River no less than the Rhine and the Thames. All the products of the mind meet and mingle from one end of the world to the other. A choice must be made between an abominable confusionism and the spiritual unity of Christian culture with all the rigorous discipline, discernment and hierarchy involved in that unity. It is to the eventual restoration of that spiritual unity of Christendom that all the ardent desires of the Church of Christ at present tend, because the message of redemption is addressed to all men and because that message must be delivered.

Whatever philologists may say and even M. Lévy-Bruhl, now duly refuted,[3] man is everywhere essentially the same, his mental and affective structure is found to be essentially identical in all climates, according to the formal testimony of missionaries,

[3] Cf. M. Olivier Leroy's *La raison primitive* (Geuthner, Paris, 1927).

whether in the case of so-called primitive peoples or peoples of the most highly refined civilization, such as the Chinese. I gladly recall in this connection the observation of M. Meyerson, one of the most eminent of modern French philosophers of science, that "reason is catholic."

And above reason the Church again unites all mankind in a transcendent and divine unity, which is the unity of the kingdom of Heaven, of the very life of God shared on this earth, and, if I may say so, of the universe of the Incarnation; and it is because it is sustained from above by that supernatural unity of the life of grace that the natural unity of reason succeeds in producing its fruit.

May I be permitted to observe once more:

"The Church is universal because she is born of God, all nations are at home in her, the arms of her crucified Master are stretched above all races, above all civilizations. She does not bring nations the benefits of civilization, but the Blood of Christ and supernatural Beatitude. . . . Therefore she reminds us that her missionaries must renounce every worldly interest, every concern with national propaganda, must know nothing but Christ, and that they are sent to found churches which shall be self-sufficient, complete with clergy. She does not profess that all races and nations have the same historical vocation and a similar human development; she does maintain in the most significant manner that they are all called of God, all alike included in her charity, that each has its legitimate place in the spiritual unity of Christendom and is capable of providing the flock of Christ with bishops." [4]

Such a dual unity, dual catholicity of reason and grace, of the human spirit and the Church, needs an intellectual instrument to manifest, consolidate and diffuse it.

At a time when East and West are exchanging all their dreams and aberrations, when all the scourges which came near to proving the undoing of Europe—scientism, atheism, modernism, the religion of inevitable Progress and the apotheosis of man—are exported by Europe and afflicting Africa and Asia like so many gospels of destruction, when the mind in all countries is struggling against the most subtle enchantments of the philosophers of this world, are we to believe that Christian culture is under no obligation itself to employ a perfectly equipped intelligence, a tried and tested doctrine? It is the most highly developed and most perfect form of Christian philosophy, the lofty wisdom under the ægis of the common Doctor of the Church which provides it with such an indispensable instrument.

"That wisdom must be made to yield, in appropriate forms of presentation and by thorough sift-

4 *The Things that are not Caesar's,* pp. 95-96.

ing to meet the genuine requirements of every several problem, the intellectual values which every country in the world needs. It is the form which preserves whatever is universal and permanent, it alone can revive the West, give it back the free and living use of its spiritual riches, its tradition and culture; it alone can also save the inheritance of the East and reconcile the two halves of the world." [5]

I beg leave to quote an example. M. Louis de la Vallée Poussin, the eminent historian of Buddhism, drew attention recently to the work performed in India by Père Dandoy and his associates.

"They publish a little paper in Bengal which is extremely well turned out, called *Christ, the Light of the World,*[6] and in which they explain how a transition is possible, nay logically inevitable, from the Vedanta, the traditional philosophy of India, to Christianity. They are first-rate Sanscrit scholars and study in lucid notes the five or six forms affected by that philosophy which varies, in gradations of which Indian scholars have never been able to make head or tail, between an apparently absolute monism and a theism which is too dualist to be orthodox as we conceive orthodoxy.

"Such an investigation, from the Indian point of view, is more than praiseworthy; it reveals the religious and mystical character of Indian specula-

[5] *The Things that are not Caesar's,* p. 109.
[6] Its exact title is *The Light of the East* (published from 30 Park Street, Calcutta).

tion, even such as affects the most rationalist appearance.

"From the practical point of view, I am convinced that it is piercing the joint in the armour. Saint Thomas is right as against Sankara, Ramanuja and the rest; he offers the only solution which completely solves all the knots in the problem; he reconciles, by transcending them, the opposing theses of Vedantic schools; he is, in a word, the true exponent of the Vedanta. . . .

"Cultured Indians, we are told, found the German philosopher Paul Deussen's book, *Das System des Vedanta*, a poor exposition, a Vedanta made up of some imperfectly understood Sankara diluted in Schopenhauer with a dash of Hegel. . . . The investigation pursued by my friends in Bengal, on the other hand, seems to be taken very seriously by the pundits. Père Dandoy and his associates have taken great trouble to read the texts and the commentaries; you have the feeling that they know in detail—and detail is so very important—what they are talking about; they engage in no polemical controversies, they import no arguments from the West; what they do bring into play, with an exactitude of theological learning which compels my heartiest admiration and a tone of narrative, in the most elusive of subjects, which is absolutely Indian and in addition a wealth of information beyond praise, is a new and convincing commentary of the old Brahmasutras. These absolutely up-to-date apologists do not wear, as Robert de Nobili once did, the garments of the Brahmin, but have devised instead a psychology which is as subtle as you like, absolutely Thomist and yet Bengali." [7]

Such an example shows us how Saint Thomas has prepared the conceptual and rational apparatus, the metaphysical apparatus of the mind which Christian culture needs, and by means of which we may hope that it will achieve its unity in the great world.

And that is precisely the most exalted privilege of Western culture, what makes it in our eyes the most precious of all: that being fundamentally universal, adumbrated by a miracle of Providence in that strength and piety of natural reason which were characteristic of ancient Greece and Rome, and thereafter developed by the Church of Christ, it became capable of producing first a Plato and an Aristotle, then a Saint Paul and a Saint Augustine and, finally, a Saint Thomas. It is to be wished that the incomparable instrument so fashioned may be adopted and employed not only by apostles of the white but also by an élite among the coloured races,

[7] *Bulletins de la Classe des Lettres et des Sciences morales et politiques de l'Académie Royale de Belgique* ("*Indianisme*": *Discours de M. Louis de la Vallée Poussin*, 9th May, 1928).—Père de Nobili was the author of various treatises in Tamil and Sanscrit expounding the Christian philosophy—and the arguments of St. Thomas—in the guise of Hindu speculation. For example, criticizing in his treatise on the soul, *Attumanirunayam*, the doctrine of transmigration, "he contrasts with perfect ease the Aristotelian concept of form, the *principium vitae*, with the brahminical idea of the soul imprisoned in the body like a bird in a cage: 'When a man dwells in a house, does the house grow up along with him? When he is not at home, does the house fall to bits?' All through the book brahminical fables and legends are found woven into the woof of the argument" (cf. Pierre Dahmen, *Un Jésuite brahme, Robert de Nobili*, Bruges, 1925).

who will learn the lesson taught by Saint Thomas as we Gauls, Celts or Germans have learned the lesson of Aristotle. In this respect the intellectual co-operation among Catholics before referred to is more than ever a pressing necessity.

But let it be well understood: nothing solid, nothing permanent, will ever be achieved without such recourse to the wisdom of Saint Thomas. It would be a tremendous illusion to think that in order to realize the task of unity more rapidly it were proper to jettison the whole inheritance of truths acquired at such a fearful price on the banks of the West. For it is precisely that inheritance which the world needs; it is the dispersion of it throughout the world which will unite the world. It must not be jettisoned but mobilized. And to mobilize it is not an easy matter, for the solution of all the new problems raised is not to be found ready-made in Saint Thomas: a new and original effort is required to disengage such a solution, an effort necessitating as much boldness in application to reality as fidelity to the most elementary principles of the master.

Not every philosophy is fit for baptism as it stands. It must first be corrected and in most cases transformed. And in many cases all that can be done is to destroy it. The reason why Aristotle could be baptized by Saint Thomas is that his metaphysical principles were based upon objective reality.

And if the great metaphysical systems of ancient civilization differ from modern systems in having *being* for their object, and are therefore capable of being universally adopted, by that very fact they have a sort of longing, as it were, to be corrected by Aristotelianism and Thomism. How much more gratifying it would be to our indolence, how much more soothing to our spirit of adventure, what a relief to play truant and to dispense with the discipline of the *philosophia perennis!* But culture cannot dispense with such a discipline, and will never more be able to dispense with Aristotle the Greek transfigured by the Angelic Doctor.

I do not say that the wisdom of Saint Thomas must be imposed as a dogma. The Gospel is not bound up with such wisdom. Nor do I say that all that is to be retained of the spiritual treasures of the East is what may have already been literally formulated in a system thenceforth deemed to be complete. The case is quite the reverse! What I say is that out of regard and respect for such treasures, and so that they shall assume their proper dimensions, and to co-operate loyally in preserving them against the forces of destruction, those who desire to integrate them in a permanent cultural achievement must equip themselves with an indefectible doctrinal apparatus.

And Thomist philosophy itself will be the better

therefor. It will emerge from the everlasting controversies of the School, it will run the highways,
take the air. What Saint Dominic said with regard
to men is equally applicable to ideas: "Grain rots in
the heap but is fruitful when sown." Thomist philosophy in itself is a progressive and assimilative
philosophy, a missionary philosophy, a philosophy
constantly at the service of primary Truth. And
Saint Thomas is not a relic of the Middle Ages, a
mere object for the consideration of history and
erudition. He is in all the fulness of the expression
the Apostle of our time.

All religions other than the Catholic religion are
in more or less narrow and servile fashion, according
as their metaphysical level is high or low, integral
parts of certain definite cultures, particular to
certain ethnic climates and certain historical forma-
tions. Only the Catholic religion, because it is supernatural and proceeds from the riven Heart of God
dying upon the cross, is absolutely and rigorously
transcendental, supra-cultural, supra-racial and
supra-national.

That is one sign of its divine origin. It is also
one of the signs of contradiction which until the
end of time will be a cause of the passion of the
Church, raised like her Master between earth and
sky. It is conceivable from this point of view that

the world is entering a phase of particularly stern conflicts which may, perhaps, be compared to the conflicts of apostolic times in the Rome of the Cæsars. On the one hand the non-Christian nations are incapable of distinguishing between their autochthonous culture, with all its human values in themselves deserving of respect and filial piety, and the errors and superstitions of their religions. And Christian universalism will have to show them how such a distinction can be made and how the Gospel respects and superelevates—and by slow degrees transforms—such particular values. The demonstration is, as a rule, not unattended with bloodshed. And the imbecile dogma of positivist sociologism, which is taught in all countries in the name of European science and according to which every religion is merely the specific product of the social clan (and Christianity therefore a specific product of the European races) will not make it any the easier.

On the other hand, when faith and charity decrease among the majority in the Christian nations, many people come to think that, because Christianity was the vivifying principle of their historical culture, it is essentially bound, enfeoffed to it. Certain apostles of Latinity (I bear it no grudge, let me assure them) are convinced—the remark was made to me one day—that our religion is a Græco-

Latin religion. Such an enormity is full of significance. Not realizing from what spirit they derive
and oblivious of the divine transcendence of what
constitutes the life of their life, they end in practice
by worshipping the true God in the same fashion
as the Ephesians worshipped Diana and primitive
man worships the idols of his tribe. Christian universalism will have to remind them that the Gospel
and the Church, without injuring any particular
culture or the State or the nation, yet dominates
them all in a pure unsullied independence and subordinates them to the eternal interests of the human
being, to the law of God and the charity of Christ.
Nor is that demonstration made without resistance.

One point should, I think, here be emphasized. If
the Kingdom of God, for the extension of which we
are bound unceasingly to labour, belongs to the
spiritual order,[8] that is to say, to the order of eternal
and supernatural life beginning on this earth, what
we describe as civilization or culture [9] belongs, on

[8] To the spiritual order *par excellence,* that is to say the supernaturally
spiritual order.

[9] The words are practically synonymous in the vocabulary of French
philosophers, whereas many German and Russian thinkers draw a distinction
between *civilization* and *culture* and use the former, conceived in a pejorative
sense, to signify a development of social life which is in the first place
material. In the sense in which I understand it, a civilization is truly deserving of the name only if it is a culture, a truly human and therefore mainly
intellectual, moral, and spiritual, development, taking the word spiritual in
its widest acceptation. [What we French and English understand by *culture,*
the Germans translate less appropriately as *Bildung,* which again suggests

the contrary, to the temporal order, directly refers to a common good which is assuredly not only material but also and in the first place intellectual and moral, although in itself of the natural order; culture and civilization, while ordered to the Kingdom of God, which superelevates them even in their own order and from which they are bound to receive their supreme rule and standard, are in direct relation to that perishable life and to the development of human nature on this earth.

This is the reason why in a world ravaged by sin, cultures and civilizations are naturally in opposition and at war.

In speaking therefore of Christian culture and its unity, what we really mean is the super-elevation produced by Christianity in the various individual ethnic and historical cultures and impressing them, while still preserving their variety intact, with an image of the supra-cultural unity of the mystical Body of Christ.

---

another idea. What we understand by *civilization* they term *Kultur*, which according to W. von Humboldt (*Über die Verschiedenheit des menschlichen Sprachbaus*, § 4) "adds Science and Art to social conditions ennobled by civilization," and is "the humanization of peoples in their external institutions and customs, and in the inner sentiments relating to these." Von Humboldt's use (c. 1836) of the words is still in the French and English sense, while the modern German use referred to in the text and copied by the Russians would seem to have developed before the war. Cf. the chapter from Prof. Burnet's *Higher Education and the War* (1917), reprinted in *Essays and Addresses*, London, 1929. Tr.]

In other words "civilization is the expansion of the truly human life of the State. It belongs, in itself, to the natural order: art, metaphysics, science, politics are strictly civil virtues. . . . But it can expand to the full only under the supernatural sky of the Church. . . . Christian civilization is a by-product of the Kingdom of God." [10]

The consequence is clear. A philosophy, a theology even, forms part of a culture: if they are to attain the pure universality which the natural reason itself demands—and reason illuminated by faith—it is absolutely essential that they also be super-elevated by the influence of grace, assumed by the mystical Body of Christ. So we return to a truth which seems to me essential and upon which I have already had occasion to insist:

The privileges enjoyed by the philosophy of St. Thomas are explicable only by the fact that St. Thomas is truly the common Doctor of the Church, because that philosophy (although the Church can never impose it as a dogma *de fide*, since it is a human synthesis) is the peculiar instrument of the intellectual life of the Church. It is that which

---

[10] Charles Journet. (Contrast Eduard Meyer's definition of *Kultur* as "the inherited stock of bodily and mental peculiarities, ideas, customs and social arrangements characteristic of a group of human beings, transmitted and increased from generation to generation." *Geschichte des Altertums, Einleitung,* § 4.)

maintains it in a purity which man abandoned to his own resources would find impossible; that which assures it that supreme degree of spirituality and universality which makes it truly *catholic* and keeps it from being restricted or particularized by the means it uses.

The metaphysics and theology of St. Thomas are expressed in a system of symbols, in a language and a form of exposition which are Latin, but the philosophy itself is no more bound to Latinism than to the astronomy of Aristotle or Ptolemy. It is bound to no particularity of climate, race or tradition, and therefore it alone is capable of recreating between the minds of men, in the superior light of the Gospel, a true unity of human culture, or restoring a spiritual Christendom. Its principles and all its notional springs have been tried and tested for six centuries past, cleansed and scoured of every accidental and burdensome accretion. It emerges to-day in its genuine radiant youth. It must be careful "to stand aloof in order to command," as Anaxagoras said of the νοῦς, not to let itself be particularized by any local condition whatsoever of tradition and culture or any party among its own adherents. To that end it must remain jealously attached to the superior virtues on which its integrity in the souls of men depends, and to the ministerial part it is called upon to play in regard to the Gospel and the blessed contemplation of the Church of Jesus Christ.[11]

If all that has just been said is true, it will be realized that if the Thomist synthesis offers us a means *par excellence* of achieving the unity of Christian culture, nevertheless, and by the very fact of its being a means, an instrument, it is not sufficient for such a unity. It would be a great mistake to believe that philosophical or theological science by itself alone, and considered as a principal agent, so to speak, can exercise a truly formative and rectifying influence on culture.

We must begin by Christ. It is not St. Thomas, it is Christ Who makes Christian culture; it is Christ, through the Church and through St. Thomas; through the contemplation of the Saints and the love which unites them to the agony of the Son of Man; through the labour of the theologians and the philosophers, which brings to the service of the Son of Man all the virtues of the mind and all its scattered riches.

The consequence is that the doctrine of the common Doctor will radiate over culture only at the same time as the Gospel and the Catholic Faith— the two radiances, one divine, the other human, helping each other and multiplying each other in

[11] Cf. *"Le Thomisme et la civilization"* in the *Revue de Philosophie,* March–April 1928, pp. 138–139.

accordance with the great law of the reciprocity of causes: *causae ad invicem sunt causae.*

Three philosophers were talking together, one Orthodox and two Catholics; a Russian, a German and a Frenchman; Nicholas Berdiaeff, Peter Wust and the writer. The problem we were discussing was how to reconcile two apparently contradictory facts: the fact that modern history appears to be, as Berdiaeff says, on the threshold of a new Middle Age in which the unity and universality of Christian culture will be recovered and extended this time to the whole universe, and the fact that the general trend of civilization seems to be towards the universalism of Antichrist and his iron rod rather than towards the universalism of Christ and His emancipatory law, and in any event to forbid the hope of a unification of the world in one universal Christian empire.

As far as I am concerned, my answer is as follows: I think that two immanent tendencies intersect at every point in the history of the world and affect everyone with their momentary complexes: one tendency draws upward everything in the world which participates in the divine life of the Church, which is in the world but not of the world, and follows the attraction of Christ, the Head of the human race.

The other tendency draws downward everything in the world which belongs to the Prince of the world, the head of all the wicked. History suffers these two internal strains as it moves forward in time, and human affairs are so subjected to a distention of increasing force until the fabric in the end gives way. So the cockle grows up along with the wheat; the capital of sin increases throughout the whole course of history and the capital of grace increases also and superabounds. As history draws nearer to Antichrist and suffers in all its visible structure transformations preparing the way for the advent of Antichrist, so also it draws nearer to Him Whom Antichrist precedes and Who conceals beneath that same concatenation of events in the world the holy task He continues to pursue among His own. For this reason I wrote:

"Nowadays the devil has made such a mess of everything in the system of life on earth that the world will presently become uninhabitable for anybody but Saints. The rest will drag their lives out in despair or fall below the level of man. The antinomies of human life are too exasperated, the burden of matter too oppressive; merely to exist one has to expose oneself to too many snares. Christian heroism will one day become the sole solution for the problems of life. Then as God proportions His graces to human needs and tempts nobody beyond his strength, we shall doubtless see coincident with the worst condition in human history a flowering of sanctity. . . ." [12]

In that case it is perfectly true that we are on the threshold of a new Middle Age, of a rediscovered unity and universality of Christian culture. But let it be as it may with the more or less permanent triumphs which we may hope for the Church, it will be realized that such a restoration of Christen-

[12] Cf. *The Things that are not Caesar's*, p. 80. In Père Allo's book upon the *Apocalypse*, the following observations will be found; they are, in my opinion, well deserving of attention: "If this be so [sc. if the figure 42, or 3 × 14, is a Messianic figure], the consequence is of immense importance for exegesis: *in the Apocalypse, the duration of the power of evil on earth is represented by a Messianic figure.* In other words, the earthly phase of the Kingdom of God, the phase of the conquests of the Gospel, is sufficiently coincident with the last and most desperate efforts of Satan to prevent the coming of that Kingdom. What we had already dimly perceived in regard to 3 ½—the time of persecution and the ministry of Christ—finds singular confirmation in 42. [The number of 'persecution time,' the space between June 168, and December 165 B.C., during which the Jews suffered under Antiochus Epiphanes as foretold by *Daniel* vii, 25, etc., is, in apocalyptic language, 'a time, times and half a time': three years and a half, forty-two months, or 1,260 days. Tr.]

". . . Such a fusion of the most sinister prospects with the most glowing aspects of the present and the future is not in the least inadmissible *a priori*. It was not inadmissible in Jewish circles, to judge from the statements of various rabbis that the days of the Messiah were to be remarkable for more than one calamity. Khiya ben Nehemia depicts the days of the Messiah as so sad in one respect that it would be impossible to distinguish guilt from innocence (*Koheleth rabba*, xii, 1; but similar ideas are already to be found in the Talmud. Cf. Volz, pp. 62–63; Lagrange, *Le Messianisme chez les Juifs*, pp. 99–115). The idea must have been familiar also to Christians who referred to the Gospel.

". . . Besides, in our own Apocalypse itself, we have already seen the two aspects continually mingled: the beneficent Horseman, in vi, 2, goes forth to conquer spiritually *at the same time* as the other horsemen sow disaster: the elect of God, in vii, will be preserved *at the same time* as the great tribulation; etc. (xii). It is the quite simple transposition of the ὠδίνες τοῦ Μεσσίου to the preparation for the second Coming." E. B. Allo, O.P., *L'Apocalypse de Saint Jean* (Paris, Gabalda, 1921), pp. 145–146.

dom, both in the social order and in the order of the spirit, must be effected in a more and more tragically divided world.

That is to say that instead of being grouped and assembled, as in the Middle Ages, in a homogeneous and integrally Christian body of civilization, limited however to a privileged portion of the inhabited earth, it seems that the unity of Christian culture must now extend over the whole surface of the globe but, on the other hand, represent only the order and living system of Christian temporal institutions and Christian hearths disseminated throughout the nations in the great supra-cultural unity of the Church. Instead of a fortress towering amid the lands we should think then rather of a host of stars scattered in the sky. Such a unity is not thereby rendered any the less real, it is merely diffused instead of being concentrated.

Whatever be the truth in these hypotheses, my object in writing these pages is to show that St. Thomas is our predestined guide in the reconstruction of Christian culture, the steward and minister of that great blessed kingdom which the Church, in the admirable Preface to the Mass of Christ the King, describes as the kingdom of truth and life, of sanctity and grace, of justice, love and peace: *regnum veritatis et vitae, regnum sanctitatis et gratiae, regnum justitiae, amoris et pacis.*

III

THE APOSTLE OF OUR TIME

"Neque enim solivaga aut jejuna, sed valde actuosa dicenda est tantarum rerum scientia, quarum pulchritudo totum hominem ad se rapiat atque convertat."
PIUS XI, ENCYCLICAL "STUDIORUM DUCEM."

LIKE primary Truth itself, whose glare he softens to our eyes, St. Thomas makes no exception of persons; he invites to the banquet of wisdom both pupil and master, the teacher and the taught, the active and the contemplative, the secular and the regular, poets, artists, scholars, and philosophers, ay, and the man in the street, if only he will give ear, as well as priests and theologians. And his philosophy appears as the only one with energy powerful and pure enough to influence effectively not only the consecrated élite which is being educated in seminaries—it were desirable that it always sufficiently realized its frightful intellectual responsibility—but also the whole universe of culture; to restore the human mind to order and so, with the grace of God, to bring the world back to the paths of Truth, the abandonment of which is likely to involve the dissolution of the world.

The disease afflicting the modern world is in the first place a disease of the mind; it began in the mind, it has now attacked the roots of the mind. Is it surprising that the world should seem to us shrouded in darkness? *Si oculus tuus fuerit nequam, totum corpus tuum tenebrosum erit.*

Just as at the moment when the original sin was committed all the harmony of the human being was shattered, because the order that insists that the reason shall be subject to God had first been violated, so at the root of all our disorders there is apparent, in the first place and above all, a rupture in the supreme ordinations of the mind. The responsibility of philosophers in this respect is enormous. In the sixteenth century, and more particularly in the age of Descartes, the interior hierarchies of the virtue of reason were shattered. Philosophy abandoned theology to assert its own claim to be considered the supreme science, and, the mathematical science of the sensible world and its phenomena taking precedence at the same time over metaphysics, the human mind began to profess independence of God and being. Independence of God; that is to say, of the supreme Object of all intelligence, Whom it accepted only half-heartedly until it finally rejected the intimate knowledge of Him supernaturally procured by grace and revelation. Independence of being; that is to say, of the con-natural

object of the mind as such, against which it ceased
to measure itself humbly, until it finally undertook to deduce it entirely from the seeds of geo-
metrical clarity which it conceived to be innate in
itself.

We have difficulty in realizing that the ordered
relation of the mind to its object should be thus
shattered; we have difficulty in realizing—so material have we become—the frightful significance,
sodden with blood and tears, of those few abstract
words; we have difficulty in realizing the tremendous upheaval, the tremendous invisible catastrophe,
thereby indicated. The mind is that "divine" activity,
as Aristotle said, that prodigy of light and life, that
supreme glory and perfection of created nature,
through which we become immaterially all things,
through which we shall one day possess our supernatural beatitude, the cause of all our actions on
earth so far as they are human actions and of the
rectitude of everything we do. Can we conceive
what is the meaning for man of the disturbance of
that life, which he carries in him and in which the
divine light has its share? The revolution inaugurated by Descartes and continued by the philosophers of the eighteenth and nineteenth centuries,
which merely let loose the destructive forces for
ever active in the minds of the children of Adam,
is an infinitely greater historical cataclysm than the

most formidable upheavals of the crust of the earth or the economy of the nations.

Indocile to the object, to God, to being, the mind becomes also and to the same extent indocile to all human authority, a rebel against all tradition and spiritual continuity. It retires within its shell, shuts itself up in the incommunicability of the individual. And if you consider that *docibilitas*, the faculty of being taught, is an essential characteristic of the created mind—nay, rather of animal faculties themselves, inasmuch as they imitate and prepare the mind, so much so that Aristotle classifies animals according to that criterion, placing those that refuse to be taught on the lowest rung; if you also consider that such *docibilitas* is in our case the real root of social life—man being a political animal primarily because he needs other men to make progress in the work of the speculative and practical reason, which is his specific work—the inevitable conclusion is, on the one hand, that by losing its docility to human teaching and its docility also to the object, the mind in our time has proceeded in the direction of an absolutely brutal hardening and a progressive weakening of reason; and, on the other hand, that the most profound and at the same time most human bonds of social life must have simultaneously become by an unavoidable consequence gradually loosened and undone.

Three main symptoms of the disease afflicting the mind at the present day down to its very roots may be discerned at the point of evolution which speculation has reached since the great changes inaugurated by the Cartesian reform.

The mind imagines that it is giving proof of its own native strength by denying and rejecting as science first theology and then metaphysics; by abandoning any attempt to know the primary Cause and immaterial realities; by cultivating a more or less refined doubt which is an outrage both to the perception of the senses and the principles of reason, that is to say the very things on which all our knowledge depends. Such a presumptuous collapse of human knowledge may be described in one word: agnosticism.

The mind at the same time refuses to recognize the rights of primary Truth and repudiates the supernatural order, considering it impossible—and such a denial is a blow at all the interior life of grace. That may be described in a word as naturalism.

Lastly, the mind allows itself to be deceived by the mirage of a mythical conception of human nature, which attributes to that nature conditions peculiar to pure spirit, assumes that nature to be in each of us as perfect and complete as the angelic nature in the angel and therefore claims for us, as being in justice our due, along with complete domination over nature, the superior autonomy, the full self-sufficiency, the αὐτάρχεια appropriate to pure forms. That may be described as individualism, giving the word its full metaphysical meaning, although *angelism* would be a more accurate description; such a term is justified by historical no less than by doctrinal considerations, because the ideal origin and metaphysical type of modern individualism are to be found in the Cartesian confusion between substance of whatever sort and the angelic monad.

I say that these three great errors are the symptoms of a really radical disease, for they attack the very root, the triple root, rational, religious and moral, of our life.

They were, to begin with, singularly latent and dissimulated, in the state of pure spiritual intentions. They are before us to-day, sparkling, oppressive, ubiquitous. Everybody sees and feels them, because their sharp unsparing point has passed from the mind into the very flesh of humanity.

Let it be observed once more, it is the integrity of natural reason, the singleness of the eye of the mind, to adapt the expression in the Gospel, the fundamental rectitude of common sense which is outraged by such errors. What a strange fate has befallen rationalism! Men emancipated themselves from all control to conquer the universe and reduce all things to the level of reason. And in the end they come to abandon reality, no longer dare to make use of ideas to adhere to being, forbid themselves the knowledge of anything beyond the sensible fact and the phenomenon of consciousness, dissolve every object of speculation in a great fluid jelly called Becoming or Evolution, conceive themselves barbarous if they do not suspect every first principle and every rational demonstration of naïveté, substitute for the effort of speculation and logical discernment a sort of refined play of instinct, imagination, intuition, visceral emotions, have lost the courage to form a judgment.

Now it is important to realize that nothing below the level of the mind can remedy this disease, which affects the mind and derives from the mind: the mind alone can cure itself. If the mind is not saved, nothing will be saved. However ailing it may be, it always conceals in its depths an essential vitality which nothing can injure or corrupt, and always remains, in the metaphysical order, the most exalted faculty of the human being. Because of the indefectible energy of its spiritual nature, the disease that afflicts it, however radical it may be, is still of the accidental order, of the operative order, and is incapable of affecting its essential constitution; and it is precisely when that disease has become most manifest that one is entitled to hope for the salutary reaction; only let it become conscious of the disease and it will immediately rouse itself against it.

It is useless, however, to be constantly finding fault: we are faced with an ineluctable necessity. The evils afflicting us have spread so far in the substance of humanity, have wrought such general havoc, that every means of defence and every extrinsic support, due in the first place to the fabric of society, to established institutions, to the moral order of the family and the State—and truth no less than the highest acquisitions of culture is in vital need of them among men—are, if not actually destroyed, at any rate shaken to their foundation. Everything which was humanly solid is compromised, "the mountains slide and leap." Man stands alone before the ocean of being and the transcendentals. It is an abnormal state for human nature and as perilous as can be. But it is at all events proof that everything henceforth depends on the restoration of the mind. The metaphysical truths which Pascal thought too remote for the common feeling of mankind are henceforth beyond a doubt the sole refuge and safeguard of the common life and the most immediate interests of humanity. It is no longer a question of wagering heads or tails. It is a question of judging, truth or falsehood, and affronting eternal realities.

The attempts at political and social reconstruction, amid the universal disorder, which the instinct of preservation urges the nations to make, will merely degenerate into a brutal and ephemeral despotism, will be incapable of producing anything stable, if the mind is not restored; the movement of religious revival apparent in the world will be permanent and truly efficacious, only if the mind is restored. Truth in the first place; *veritas liberabit vos*. Woe betide us, if we fail to realize that now as in the days of the creation of the world, the Word is in the beginning of the works of God.

What is the most striking characteristic of that which is most exalted, most divine, most efficacious in St. Thomas Aquinas, the most striking characteristic of the very sanctity of St. Thomas? "The chief characteristic of the sanctity of St. Thomas is what St. Paul calls '*sermo sapientiae*, the word of wisdom,' and the union of the two forms of wisdom, the acquired and the infused. . . ."[1] Let us say that the sanctity of St. Thomas is the sanctity of the mind; and I wish I could vividly convey all the reality contained in those words.

Not only does the *philosophy* of St. Thomas maintain better than any other the rights and nobility of the mind—affirming its natural pre-eminence over the will; gathering under its light all the hier-

[1] Pius XI, Encyclical *Studiorum Ducem*.

archized diversity of being; itself identifying it, when it finds it in pure act, with the infinitely holy nature of the living God; unceasingly reminding us in the practical order that the life of man, and the Christian life pre-eminently "are based upon the mind"—but also, and this goes ever so much further, the very *sanctity* of Thomas Aquinas, his charity, his sacrifice of praise, his consummation in Jesus, are all accomplished and radiant in him at the summit of the spirit, in that life of the mind which Aristotle declared to be superior to human life, where the activity of man borders on the activity of pure forms; and it is thence that everything pours out in waves of light, down to the lowliest faculties of the created being. That is the sense in which we should understand the age-old title of *Doctor Angelicus,* so appropriately bestowed on Thomas Aquinas. St. Thomas is in a super-eminent sense the pure intellectual, because the intellect itself is his means *par excellence* of serving and loving God, because the intellect itself is the host which he adores.

His chief work, every schoolboy knows, was, with the approbation and encouragement, nay, rather at the instigation, of the papacy, to make room in the Christian mind for Aristotle, by completing and perfecting him, by purging him of all accretions, and for all the natural wisdom of the phi-

117

losophers whom Tertullian called "glorious animals." [2] He fought a very hard fight to achieve it. For if there is between Aristotle and the Gospel, between human wisdom which grew up on the soil of Greece and revelation which came down from the sky of Judæa, a pre-established harmony which is in itself an admirable apologetic symbol, nevertheless, to realize that harmony, to make it actual, by triumphing over the obstacles which arose from the limitations of the human subject, all the strength of the great dumb ox of Sicily was required over and above the maturity of the civilization of St. Louis's age. As Pascal saw so clearly, it is the mediocrity of our intellectual capacity in the first place which makes us fall into error, because we are incapable of comprehending simultaneously apparently opposite truths which are in reality complementary. "Exclusion" is thus "the cause of heresy" and more generally of error. The self-styled Augustinians of the thirteenth century, confusing, in their material attachment to the literal interpretation of their master, the formal objects of faith and reason, of metaphysical wisdom and the wisdom of the saints —inclining, in short, to what we should nowadays describe as anti-intellectualism—what else were they doing, after all, but denying the rights of truth

[2] *De Anima*, I (Reifferscheid-Wissowa, p. 299, l. 10). Cf. *Adversus Marcionem*, I, xiii.

in the natural order? That tendency culminated
later in formal heresy, with Luther and his inhuman
hatred of reason. The Averroists who, in their fa-
natical devotion to an Aristotle corrupted by the
Arabs, were incapable of perceiving the peculiar
light and the supremacy of faith and theology—
inclining, in short, to rationalism—denied the rights
of supernatural truth; and we know only too well
where that tendency was to culminate. St. Thomas
shattered them both, and he will shatter them again,
for it is always the same battle. And at the same
time he determined by conclusive principles the
rational theory of that distinction and harmony
between the natural and the supernatural orders
which are essentially dear to the Catholic Faith and
more important to the life of the world than the
cycle of the stars and the seasons.

But that double battle against the Averroists and
the old belated Scholasticism, that immense achievement of integrating Aristotle in Catholic philosophy, is merely the manifestation and the indication
of an interior struggle, still greater and more formidable. The peculiar task of St. Thomas, the undertaking to which he was appointed by the Lord, was
to bring the proudest and most intractable (because the most spiritual) of powers—I mean the
mind, in all its apparel of riches and majesty, armed
with all its speculative energies, all its logic and

science and art, all the harness of its fierce virtues which are rooted in being itself—to bring the mind (by compelling it to sobriety but never to abdication) whole and entire into the holy light of Christ, to the service of the Child-God lying in the manger between the ox and the ass. He has all the Magi behind him for the rest of time.

Such considerations enable us, I think, to catch a glimpse of the mystery of the very vocation of St. Thomas. A very surprising vocation, it has often been observed. For the place which Thomas Aquinas was called upon to leave in obedience to the summons received from God was not the world, but the cloister, not the society of his time, but Monte Cassino. It was not what the Church calls the ignominy of the habit of the world, *ignominia saecularis habitus,* but the holy Benedictine habit which he discarded to don the white robe of St. Dominic. It was not the danger of the world that he quitted for the state of perfection: he moved from one state of perfection to another, and a more difficult one. He had to leave the house of the Blessed Father Benedict from whom, as a little oblate in a black habit, he had learned the twelve degrees of humility [3] and of whom, as a Doctor, dazzled with ecstasy

[3] As Père Petitot very justly observes, St. Thomas, who had read to him daily a passage from the *Collationes* of Cassian, may be said to have remained imbued to the marrow with Benedictine spirituality, so little introverted, so careless of 'psychology.'

after the completion of his work, he asked hospitality in order to die. And knowing that such was the pleasure of the Lord, he persisted in taking his departure with all the tenacity of an indomitable will.

Brothers, mother, prison, guile and violence, nothing could shake his determination. Why was he so obstinate? He had to be about his Father's business. What is God? He had to teach us the spelling of divine things, and that was what Countess Theodora could not understand.

St. Dominic had asked St. Benedict for him in Heaven, because the Word of God had asked St. Dominic for him, to entrust him with a mission to the Christian mind. His duty was to serve the mind, but as the priest serves the creature of God. His duty was to teach it, to baptize it, to nourish it with the Body of the Lord, to preside at the nuptials of the Mind and the Lamb. On the white pebble given to him, which was also the live coal that purified his lips, there was written the word *truth*.

St. Thomas is peculiarly and above all the *apostle of the mind*: that is the first reason why he is to be considered the *apostle of our time*.

The second reason is what may be described as the absolutism of truth in his soul and in his work, with the triple consequence of absolute purity in intellectual quality, absolute rigour of logic and at the same time of harmonious complexity in doctrine, and absolute docility of obedience to reality. All philosophers and theologians doubtless seek and desire truth. But do they desire it with such vehemence and so exclusively? not to mention particularist preoccupations and other vices of all kinds, vanity, curiosity, the vain desire for originality and novelty pursued for their own sakes, which so often spoil the quest, may not a philosopher in his search for truth address himself *also* to something else? It is in reality very rare for Truth *alone* to attract everything to itself in the heaven of the mind. Other transcendentals, giant stars, mingle their allurements also and divert speculation. And this is a grave disorder, for science as such should be regulated only by what is true. Is there not deep down in the metaphysics of Platonism, as in the theology of Scotism, a secret collusion between Beauty or the Good and Truth, between Love and Knowledge? Other philosophers are affected by more mundane influences, convenience, complaisance, conformity to the needs of the day or to the exigencies of a teaching curriculum or more generally to the frailty of the human subject—and by an ill-controlled anxiety as to the practical consequences, an effort to strike a balance between opposite opinions which is taken to be wisdom, whereas in reality it is merely the attempt to discover a *medium virtutis* between truth and error, as though truth and error were two opposite vices. So truths are diminished by the sons of men.

St. Thomas, on the other hand, leaves truth all its grandeur intact, and its grandeur is to be estimated by the Son of God. He is a philosopher and a theologian and he knows nothing but Truth and is that not the way in which Philosophy and Theology, considered as such, must know nothing but Jesus crucified? He finds his whole standard of regulation in being, he is in absolutely direct relation to his object. Nothing but the intelligible necessities and exigencies of the supreme principles ever determines his solutions, even though they should be so rendered the more difficult for us, even though they should make men exclaim: *durus est hic sermo.* And if his doctrine is based entirely, in the analytical order, *in via inventionis,* on the idea of being, the primary datum of the mind, it is nevertheless entirely suspended, in the synthetic order, *in via judicii,* from the idea of God, of primary Truth, the supreme object of every mind.[4] St. Thomas cast his net upon the universe and carried off all things, transformed into life in the mind, towards the beatific vision. This theology of the pacific is, under the

[4] Cf. Père Garrigou-Lagrange, *"La première donnée de l'intelligence"* in *Mélanges thomistes,* 1923.

light of faith, an immense movement of speculation between two intuitions, the intuition of being and the first principles of reason, whence it takes its departure and which is granted to it on this earth, and the intuition of God clearly perceived, towards which it proceeds and which will be granted to it later. Ordering the whole discourse to an ineffable supreme end, it remains perpetually rational, but at the same time teaches reason not to look for its standard in itself and in face of the mysteries below, such as matter and potentiality; just as in face of the mysteries above, such as the influence of divine premotion on created liberty, it asks us to do homage to the rights of being over our spirit as to the divine sublimity. That is the reason why it is so serene and universal, so open and so free, most boldly affirmative and humbly prudent, most systematic and least partial, most intractable and hospitable to every delicate shade of difference in reality, richest in certitudes and yet most sedulously careful to make allowance for probabilities and opinions, most resolute and uncompromising and most detached from human knowledge. So transcendent is the object in which its ardent desire is to lose itself!

Now I say that in this respect also St. Thomas answers in a special fashion the needs of the present time. The spirit nowadays is exposed to such extreme dangers that no palliative can possibly be sufficient for it. Many compromises which might formerly have been successful are now utterly futile to help minds ploughed to their very depths by modern controversies and the more exacting therefore in their criticisms.

To mention only philosophy, this is specially apparent when you come to consider certain primary questions such as the distinction between essence and existence, or the analogy of being, or the nature of intellection, or the value of the intuition of exterior sensibility, or the relation of pre-eminence between the mind and the will.

The work of the negative forces makes such rapid progress at the present day that an inexorably rigorous philosophy is required to get the better of it, one so comprehensive at the same time that it can do justice to all the diversities in which contemporary speculation, for lack of a controlling light, exhausts itself. So it comes about that what is most apt to our needs is precisely the absolutism of truth, what is most opportune and "practical" is doctrinal radicalism, but a radicalism devoid of all narrowness and brutality, all partiality and fanaticism, and suspended therefore from the only true Absolute, from the transcendence of primary Truth, whence all things proceed in being. A thousand doctrines can aggravate the state of the mind, only one can cure it.

Thomism—and this is the third reason why St. Thomas should be described as the apostle of our time—is alone capable of delivering the mind from the radical errors mentioned in the beginning of this chapter.

Scrutinizing knowledge metaphysically, while respecting—it is the only system which does so—the original nature and mysterious immateriality of knowledge, placing our ideas in continuity with things through the intuition of the senses and resolving all our learning in the evidence of being and first principles, whose transcendental value enables it to ascend to God, the philosophy of St. Thomas is a form of wisdom sufficiently exalted to save the mind from the enchantments of agnosticism and to counter the devil of idealism (already far advanced in age) with a realism which is not naïve but soundly critical.

Conscious of the infinite elevation and the infinite liberty of the Creator, as of the radically contingent basis of the created being, assuring, through a sound conception of the universal, the value of nature and its laws, and pointing out that nature still remains in the sight of God immensely ductile and immensely perfectible—penetrable throughout by the divine influence—it reduces to absurdity the naturalist postulate and the metaphysical hypocrisy which, concealed behind the curtain of the positive sciences, attempts to endow the creature with the aseity of divinity.

Understanding all the grandeur and servitude involved in the very idea of rational animal, placing the human mind on the lowest rung of the ladder of spirits, abruptly dismissing all its pretensions to play at being pure spirit, making proper allowance for the autonomy which becomes us as spirits and the dependence which becomes us as creatures, as material creatures and as wounded creatures, it destroys by the root, by its *angelist* root, an individualism which in reality sacrifices human personality to an illusory and devouring image of man.

The reason is that St. Thomas—and this is the most immediate benefit he confers—brings the mind back to its object, orientates it towards its end, restores it to its nature. He tells it that it is made for being. How could it possibly not give ear? It is as though you were to tell the eye that it is made for seeing or the wings that they are made for flying. It is itself it rediscovers when it finds its object; it orders itself entirely to being; in accordance with the sovereign inclination which things have for their first principle, it tends, above all, to subsisting Being itself.

Simplicity of perception is at the same time restored to it; artificial obstacles no longer obtrude to make it hesitate before the natural evidence of first principles and the continuity between philosophy and common sense is re-established.

Submissive to the object, but in order to attain its true liberty, because it is in such submission that it acts with the most spontaneous and living activity; docile to the teaching of masters, but in order to make its own grasp of the object more intense and complete, because it is for the love of being that it invites the labour of the ages to succour and fortify it, it restores within itself its own essential hierarchies and the order of its virtues.

What constitutes the nobility of philosophers, of modern philosophers in particular, is that in spite of their aberrations they are genuinely devoted to the mind, even when they ruin it. But their devotion to the mind has for the most part been greater than their love of God. St. Thomas loves God more than the mind, but his devotion to the mind is greater than the devotion of all the other philosophers. That is the reason why he can restore it, by reminding it of its duties. He shames it out of its cowardice, gives it back the courage to affront the supreme truths. He shames it out of its vain glory, forces it to measure itself against things and to listen to a tradition. He teaches it again simultaneously the two complementary virtues it had lost together, magnanimity and humility.

The apostle of the mind, the doctor of truth, the
restorer of the intellectual order, St. Thomas wrote
not for the thirteenth century but for our time. His
own time is the time of the spirit, which dominates
the ages. I say that he is a contemporary writer, the
most modern of all philosophers. He adheres so
purely to the high light of wisdom that as regards
the inferior sciences and their moving shadows he
enjoys such liberty as no philosopher ever knew: all
the sensible vesture borrowed from the science of
the thirteenth century may be discarded, his philosophical and metaphysical doctrine remains as intact as the soul once it has departed from the body.
And the divestiture effected by the revolutions
which have taken place in the science of phenomena
since the time of Nicole Oresme, Leonardo da Vinci
and Galileo, was perhaps necessary to bring Thomism to the state of spirituality, and therefore of ef-
fectiveness, truly corresponding to the spiritual elevation of the authentic thought of St. Thomas. He
stands at the cross-roads before us; he holds the key
to the problems which oppress our hearts; he teaches
us how to triumph over anti-intellectualism and
rationalism alike, over the disease which depresses
the reason below the level of reality and the disease
which exalts it above that level; he communicates
to us the secret of true humanism, of the supreme

development of human personality and the intellectual virtues, but in sanctity, not in concupiscence, through the spirit and the cross, not through the grandeurs of the flesh. At a time sorely tormented by the desire (too frequently diffuse, exhausting itself in the things of this world), for a kingdom of the heart and a life of love, he teaches the only doctrine which affirms the absolute practical primacy of charity in our life and which invites us to the banquet of true love, of supernatural charity, I mean, yet without repudiating the mind and its metaphysical superiority or adulterating charity itself by contaminating it with pragmatism, humanitarianism or animal sensibility. Charity should always increase in virtue of the first commandment, and the perfection of charity for this reason falls under the commandment, as the end to which everyone is bound to tend according to his condition. Such is the law of gravitation that the Angelic Doctor teaches to a world all the more haunted by the idea of progress because it is ignorant for the most part of the meaning of progress.

William of Tocco even in his day dwelt unceasingly upon the *modernity* of Friar Thomas. That modernity is in truth at opposite poles to the modernity pursued nowadays and found so captivating. For St. Thomas is only accidentally an innovator; his one desire is the truth: whereas innovations are made nowadays for the sake of novelty as such, and truth has become a mere accident. Such being the case, the object is not so much to improve what is old as to destroy it and to exalt the originality of every thinking subject rather than to make thought conform to the object. It is a complete reversal of the proper order, an essentially particularist and negative method, which is in reality essentially retrograde. All acquired truths are thus inevitably bound to be annihilated one after the other.

The method practised by St. Thomas is, on the contrary, essentially universalist and positivist. Its object is to preserve all the acquired knowledge of humanity in order to add to and perfect it; and it involves the more and more absolute effacement of the philosopher before the truth of the object. If he devotes himself to Aristotle, it is not because he considers Aristotle a fashionable philosopher, recently imported by the Arabs, but because he recognized him to be the best interpreter of natural reason, the philosopher who based philosophy on foundations in conformity with what is. And he follows him, yet criticizing him at every step, correcting and purifying him by a higher light, which is not the light of Aristotle but of incarnate Wisdom. If he opposes the too materialist disciples of St. Augustine, it is not for the purpose of destroying St. Augustine, but with the object of following and

131

understanding him in a more vivid, more profoundly faithful, manner, in a more perfect commerce of spirit. And no theologian was ever more
sedulously devoted to the common secular wisdom
with which the Church is divinely instructed. That
is the reason why the Angelic Doctor is also the
Common Doctor of the Church. The Common
Doctor! What an admirable title, indicative of a
truly superhuman grandeur, a title which puts all
our sorry vanities in their place and answers the
most pressing needs of the moment! It is not a special Doctor or a particular Doctor or an original
Doctor, or a Doctor peculiar to our person or our
family, it is not an illuminate Doctor, or a devout or
subtle or irrefragable Doctor, or a Doctor *facundus*
or *resolutissimus* or *eximius,* or a *venerabilis incep-
tor,* but a Common Doctor, the Common Doctor
of the Church that we need. There he stands on the
threshold of modern times offering us in the elab-
orately ornamented basket of his thousands of arguments the sacred fruits of wisdom.

Now something very much more important is
taking place in our time than many material events
more easily noticeable. At the voice of the Church,
the philosophy of St. Thomas is not only restored or
in process of being restored in Catholic schools and
in the education of aspirants to the priesthood, but
it has also emerged from the old folios in which it

was kept in reserve, not itself old but as youthful as truth, it speaks to the world and claims its place, that is to say the first place, in the intellectual life of the age, it cries in the market-place, as it is said of wisdom: *sapientia foris praedicat, in plateis dat vocem.* After the long idealist aberration due to Descartes and the great Kantian heresy, we are now spectators of an attempt to reintegrate the philosophy of being in Western civilization. Lovers of paradox and novelty should be the first to rejoice.

An enormous task has here to be accomplished— a difficult task, not devoid of danger. But it is a splendid risk, καλὸς κίνδυνος; and should we not imitate St. Thomas also in what I described a moment ago as his modernity, in his boldness in innovating, in his intellectual courage in risking novelty? For it is perfectly true, but in a sense more subtle than the devotees of Evolution think, that wherever there is life on earth, there are movement and renewal, risks therefore to be run and unknown dangers to be affronted. It is not by revolt, however, that the greatest number of obstacles is to be surmounted but by the restoration of order; it is not for destruction that most energy is required but for construction. St. Thomas Aquinas is the hero of the intellectual order; the immense philosophical and theological enterprise which he undertook in his day and which, to be brought to a successful issue, required not only his genius but also all the prudence and energy, the whole perfect organism of the virtues and the gifts of his admirable sanctity, is a much more marvellous adventure than the finest adventures of men—an angelic adventure. He told his companions that he would never be anything in his Order or in the Church. His shoulders bore the burden of the whole future of Christian civilization and the mind and the greatest task ever imposed by the Church upon any of her children.

Well! Each of us, children though we be in comparison with such a giant, ought yet to have some share of his spirit because we are his disciples. We are certainly not childish enough to pretend, as some people invite us to do, to take modern philosophers for our masters and, adopting their principles, to treat Descartes, ay and Kant and Bergson, as St. Thomas treated Aristotle. As though one could deal with error in the same way as with truth and as though to build a house the foundations had perpetually to be changed! No, what is required of us is that, while rejecting absolutely the principles and spirit of modern philosophy—because they go so far as to equate the human creature with God—while clinging to the principles of St. Thomas with a fidelity which will never be too faithful—without admitting the least diminution or any admixture, for assimilation is possible only if the organism is

intact—we transmit the light of St. Thomas into
the intellectual life of our time, think our time in
that light, and devote ourselves to informing, animating and ordering in that light all the material,
palpitating with life and sometimes so rich with
such a precious human quality, which the world
and its art, its philosophy, science and culture, have
prepared and spoiled, alas, in the past four centuries;
that we try to preserve everything in the modern
world which still has life in it, and apprehend once
more, in order to bring them back to the perfect
order of wisdom, those moving constellations, those
spiritual milky ways, which, under the weight of
sin, are sinking into dissolution and death. Of course
I do not think that such an enterprise can ever be
completely successful; to indulge such a hope would
argue a great illusion in regard to the nature of
man and the course of his history; but what is necessary—and it is sufficient—is that the deposit be preserved and that those who love the truth may be
able to recognize it.

Nothing below the level of the mind, I said above,
can cure the mind. But what is better than the mind
on this earth, infused charity must also be enlisted.
If the return to intellectual order must be the work
of the mind itself, the mind nevertheless requires the
help, in this work which is its own, of Him Who is

the first principle of the light it sheds and Who reigns in the spirits of men only through charity; if the philosophy and theology of St. Thomas are exclusively based and firmly grounded upon the pure objective necessities which compel the assent both of natural reason and of reason enlightened by faith, the human mind is nevertheless naturally so weak and weakened still further by original sin and the speculation of St. Thomas is of such a lofty intellectuality that in fact, so far as the subject was concerned, all the supernatural graces whose assistance was guaranteed to St. Thomas by his eminent sanctity and the unique character of his mission, were necessary to enable that speculation to be transmitted to us, and it is necessary and always will be necessary, if it is to continue living unimpaired among men, that it be fortified by the superior assistance of those gifts of the Holy Ghost which are present in every Christian and which develop in us with sanctifying grace and charity.

Not to appreciate these truths would be to labour under a great delusion. They are, more particularly, made only the more urgent by the very diffusion of Thomism. A theory of wisdom, once it gains currency among men, ought to be more apprehensive of becoming one day fashionable than of the sophisms of its adversaries. Has not even the official teaching, oblivious of the famous darkness of the

Middle Ages, begun to take a serious interest in St. Thomas? I am told that an imposing number of the theses for a doctorate presented to the Sorbonne is devoted to the Thomist philosophy. We congratulate ourselves, naturally. But we do not conceal from ourselves that in proportion as minds insufficiently prepared and equipped, and more or less under the influence of modern philosophies, take to examining this philosophy, it will run the risk of being studied without the appropriate enlightenment and so be subjected to inadequate, fragmentary and distorting interpretations. The like has happened before and not in the work of donnish historians only.

How to parry this danger, we may learn from St. Thomas himself, from his philosophy and—still more efficaciously perhaps—from his example. Did he not confess to his companion Reginald that his learning had been acquired in the first place by means of prayer? Did he not, whenever he wanted to study, to debate, to write or to dictate, first have recourse to the secrecy of prayer in tears before God to be instructed in truth? Were not metaphysical wisdom and theological wisdom in his eyes but the footstool and the throne of the wisdom of the Holy Ghost? Was not this greatest of all Doctors raised to such a high degree of the mystical life that towards the end the savour of God he had en-

137

joyed in ecstasy spoiled all his inclination for human learning? Because he had perceived the eternal light too clearly, he died before he had completed his work.

Recent books have excellently described, and the Encyclical *Studiorum Ducem* has admirably shown, the combination in him of the life of study and the life of prayer. That is the secret both of his sanctity and his wisdom.

It is the secret, also, of the unique splendour of his teaching. Teaching, he tells us, is a function of the active life, and it must be confessed that the burdens and incumbrances peculiar to action are only too frequently to be encountered in it; it comports even a certain danger for the life of the spirit in the ponderous stirring of concepts which is the essence of the labour of teaching and which always runs the risk, if you are not constantly on your guard, of becoming material and mechanical.

St. Thomas was an accomplished teacher because he was ever so much more than a teacher, because his pedagogic *discourse* came down whole from the very simple heights of contemplation.

Think of him in that great disputation he held triumphantly at Paris just before Easter in 1270, on the most controverted point of his teaching, the thesis of the unicity of substantial form, against John Peckham, Regent of the Friars Minor, and later,

Archbishop of Canterbury. The bishop of Paris, the masters in theology, all the doctors were determined to ruin him. They were inflamed by jealousy or exasperated by the calm way in which he broke with hallowed routine, and their eyes darted threats, while their expression was full of menace, against him.

They had reason enough, indeed, to be disconcerted, for he was not one of them, he derived the origin of wisdom from a more exalted source than they did, from the still unruffled silence which is the father of preaching. *Nisi efficiamini sicut parvuli.* With all his learning, this great theologian, whose confession, according to the testimony of Friar Reginald, was like the confession of a child of five, stood in their midst, in his simplicity, not a defenceless, but an ingenuous simplicity, a natural (*ex Deo nata*) and not acquired simplicity, humble and severe as innocence, the image and configuration of the child Jesus amid the doctors.

Such is the way in which the Word of God is realized in him, the word which must be verified somehow or other in all Christians, and which will have wisdom given to little ones—to such as are "children in their own eyes," as it is written in the Book of Kings—and God choose "what is not" to confound "what is." For learning does not, any more than art and every superior fulness of humanity, as

some unbalanced minds of interior poverty sometimes try to persuade us, prevent the saintly soul
from being in its interior as in a genuine void, with
no self-confidence whatever, for all that apparatus
being but a pure means for it, it rests its hope in absolutely none of it. Its hope traverses the whole of
creation to base itself on God alone and it considers
absolutely none of that as a personal, possession,
confining it to its own private property.

Because he kept his whole soul attached only to
the wounds in the humanity of Christ, the portal
to the mysteries of deity, Thomas Aquinas was perfectly poor in spirit amid all the riches of the mind;
because he knew the rights, all the rights of primary
Truth, he embarked on knowledge only to make his
way to wisdom, he delivered himself unreservedly
to the Spirit of Truth. By his life and doctrine he
showed that the contemplative life is better than the
active life, and that it constitutes, when it overflows
into an apostolate, the state of life which is purely
and simply the most perfect; that the contemplation of the saints is worth more than the speculation
of the philosophers; that the loftiest intellectuality,
far from being diminished, is corroborated and carried to the summit of the spirit by the humility of
the knowledge of the Cross. St. Thomas thereby
teaches the mind the highest condition of its salvation, and for that reason also he deserves to be called

the apostle of our time, which believes that it has sacrificed so much to intellectuality, and so cruelly misconceives the conditions governing it; whose great distress is that it has forgotten the union of the intellectual and the spiritual life, and whose most profound need, more or less obscurely felt, is to recover such a union.

There is a final reason why the title of apostle of our time may be appropriately bestowed on St. Thomas Aquinas. An apostle is not only one sent into the world to preach the Word of God to the ignorant and the infidel, to convert souls to truth and so to expand the mystical body of the Saviour. He is also one who preserves and increases the faith in souls, one who is given to the Church to be a pillar, a rampart and a light therein, and to serve, in his capacity of doctor of truth, to increase her mysterious life of grace and sanctity. The absolutely unique part played from this point of view in modern times by him of whom the Church proclaims, in the prayer for his feast, that his admirable learning enlightens her, that his holy activity makes her fruitful, and whose doctrine she implores God to enable us to penetrate, *et quae docuit intellectu conspicere,* is too familiar for repetition. Now one characteristic in this respect seems to be the consummate touch as it were of the divine art, ever sedulously

141

careful to depict the features of its saints in perfect
likeness: the prince of metaphysics and sacred learning is also the doctor of the Blessed Sacrament. He
thus achieves and consummates his function of serv-
ant of the eternal Word, the Word which enlightens
the mind, the Word which is the archetype of all
splendour, the Word which became incarnate and
is hidden in our midst under the whiteness of bread.
There is the divine immensity, there the benignity
and humanity of the Truth he serves, of the Truth
which we also serve and which will have us called
not only its servants, but also its friends, *vos dixi
amicos*. It is the same Truth which is eager to give
itself to us all in light and in substance in the beatific
vision and which meanwhile gives itself in light
through doctrine and contemplation, in substance
through the Eucharist. Distributed to all, partaken
of by all, through teaching or in the sacrament, it
remains whole and unbroken. Here it gathers together the minds of men in the clarity which descends from the uncreated Word; there it unites the
mystical body of Christ in the communion of the
Body and Blood of the incarnate Word. And was it
not with one same love that Thomas watches over
its integrity in doctrine, which is the created participation of primary Truth, and adored its presence
in the Sacrament, the personification of primary Truth? He held it in his hands, that Truth he

loves, and his heart swooned for ecstasy, beholding it. And so the Pope invited him to compose for the entire Church the hymn of that great Mystery of faith; and another Pope, six centuries and a half later, bestowed on him the title of Eucharistic Doctor.

Now, is not an immense devotion to the Blessed Sacrament, preceding and enveloping devotion to the Sacred Heart, the main feature of Catholic piety in our time? Is not the feast of the *Corpus Domini* the great modern feast in the Church? While the world pursues its downward course, is not the Church, who prepares ascents in her heart, gathering souls together with a more and more pressing maternal solicitude about the Body of the Lord? Doctor of the Eucharist, St. Thomas is thus preeminently the apostle and teacher of our time. Listen to the Christian multitude singing the divine hymns which proceed from the soul and lips of the Theologian. I said a moment ago that he has all the Magi behind him. He has all the body of the faithful behind him. He carries the monstrance and walks in front of the ages.

If St. Thomas is for us all that I have said he is, with what fervour of confidence ought we not to ask him for the secret of wisdom and the apostolic conquest of the modern world? We will cling to his habit, we will not let him go until he has divulged that secret. The Church, by the voice of Peter, exhorts us to do so with extraordinary insistence. Shall we not listen to her entreaties?

If you seek for truth, she cries aloud, go to that philosophy. I show you the way; go, open your eyes, see for yourselves.

We should be sorry for those who, incapable of seeing or seeing only with the eyes of prejudice, are loath to think that their own sight may perhaps be in need of attention by study and prayer and prefer to think that it is the Church of God which has a beam in her eye.

But for such as are disposed to obey the request of the Church, and to go to school to St. Thomas, let it be observed that there are two ways of studying St. Thomas. And if it is true that man attains knowledge only on condition of first being taught, if it is true that Thomas Aquinas, the common Doctor of the Church is, after Jesus Christ, the Master *par excellence,* the ever living Master who from the heart of the beatific vision watches over his doctrine and makes it fruitful in souls, then it must be said that of the two ways of studying St. Thomas, one is sound, the other radically vicious. I am so strongly convinced of this that I should like at all costs to persuade undergraduate youth of the fact. There is a way of studying St. Thomas which consists of reading Kant, Bergson and Blondel to begin with, then the Fathers, then Avicenna and Averroes, then as occasion arises, Peter Lombard or Alexander of Hales, and finally the writings of St. Thomas in chronological order (bits of all these, of course, for life is short), so as to throw light upon St. Thomas— the light of modern philosophy—and to discern everything he received from his predecessors, everything he added to them, everything he received from himself and added to himself in the course of his individual evolutive progress. This method, taken as a rule of intellectual discipline, is useless and sterile. Because what it comes to after all is treating St. Thomas as an object to be judged—and behaving as though we were already in possession of knowledge, whereas it is a question of acquiring knowledge.

Such investigations and comparisons will be fruitful and necessary—the intensive study of modern philosophers especially—on condition that they are undertaken with the necessary illumination and are not expected to yield too much, and by such as have attained adult age in learning. But they serve only to distend *incipientes*, they provide no knowledge.

The other way is to put oneself really as regards St. Thomas in the position of a living recipient from a living donor, of one who is formed and enlightened facing one who forms and enlightens: so that St. Thomas may teach us to think and see, so that we may advance, under his guidance, to the conquest of intelligible being. This is a good and fruitful way, it puts the soul in the truth of its own condition, to lead it to the truth of things.

If we adhere to such a method faithfully, it will develop in us a profound love for the vivifying thought of St. Thomas and the actual text, far superior to any commentary, in which that thought is transmitted to us with marvellous limpidity and a special grace, as it were, of light and simplicity. It will teach us to study that text as a whole and in the order of the articles. It will teach us also, by the progressive development itself of the Thomist *habit*,[5] to make a proper use of the great commentators and to discern the formal line of the authentic tradition we need to attain to a perfect understanding of so exalted a doctrine. For the mind of St. Thomas is singularly vast and profound: to penetrate its essential vitality and to meet the fresh difficulties which have arisen in course of time, is the text by itself, precious and illuminating though it be, sufficient for our instruction? Do we not need further explanation through the movement and progress characteristic of every animate organism, of the hidden

[5] On the meaning to be given to this word, cf. *Art and Scholasticism*, p. 150, note 6.

articulations and inflexible hierarchy of the theses controlling that immense spiritual universe? And if it is true, as Plato says, that the written word, being incapable of defending and explaining itself unaided, always needs the help of its father, shall we believe that God, when He created St. Thomas, did not give him, in a living tradition, the means of coming to the help of his philosophy and communicating its spirit to us? This is the sense in which Leo XIII, while recommending us in the Encyclical *Aeterni Patris* to study in the first place the doctrine of St. Thomas in the living spring itself, *ex ipsis ejus fontibus,* advised us also to drink from the streams of clear and limpid water which flowed from that spring, *rivi integri et illimes,* as opposed to other tributaries swollen with alien and noxious waters, *rivi qui exinde fluxisse dicuntur, re autem alienis et non salubribus aquis creverunt.*

But all our personal talents, all the human help of tradition, and the assistance of all the commentators and expositors will be of no avail, if that which is the object and the end of the mind, the goal of its natural inclination, is not also the object and the goal of our voluntary inclination, of the desire which moves us wholly towards our good, will profit us nothing, if we do not love the truth with our whole heart, if we do not exert ourselves to love the truth as he himself loved it, that great Doctor whose tranquil eyes were wet with tears, so weary was his heart with waiting for the vision.

If we love the truth in the souls of men, if we realize the thirst in the anguish of the world, if we are ready to sacrifice everything to slake that thirst; if we love truth in the Church, if we understand the significance of Benedict XV's words, adopted by Pope Pius XI— "The Church has declared the doctrine of St. Thomas to be her own peculiar doctrine" —then we shall not be greatly deterred by scholastic difficulties; rather we may hope to participate in the light shed by St. Thomas, really to understand—*intellectu conspicere*—the things he taught, and to be of use to the best of our ability, poor though it be, in that universal task of restoration in truth entrusted to him by the Master of History.

IV

THE COMMON DOCTOR

"Quia ipse plus illuminavit Ecclesiam quam omnes alii Doctores."   JOHN XXII (1318).
"Thomae doctrinam Ecclesia suam propriam edixit esse."
BENEDICT XV (1921).

I WOULD not have the intention of this chapter misunderstood. It is merely an attempt to define the attitude adopted by the Catholic Church in regard to the philosophy of St. Thomas, leaving theology, which maintains an intrinsic and essential relation with faith, out of consideration. In publishing it I am full aware that it would be absurd to substitute the argument from authority or any kind of constraint for reasons of intrinsic evidence which alone are capable of determining scientific adhesion to a system of philosophy. The Thomist philosophy does not derive its principles or its *raison d'être* from religious faith or the authority of the Church, and it would be a great mistake to consider it as a doctrine intended for the exclusive use of ecclesiastics and religious services. It is a philosophy based solely on evidence and it lives by reason. Of itself it be-

149

longs to the same profane cycle as the liberal arts. I even think that the time has come for it to spread into every kind of profane speculative activity, to quit the confines of school, seminary or college and to assume throughout the whole world of culture the rôle appropriate to a wisdom of the natural order: its place is among its sister sciences and it must exchange ideas with politics and ethnology, history and poetry; bred in the open air, in the free discussions of peripateticism, its desire is, while holding aloof from the active business of mankind, to take an interest in everything that concerns human life, it is essential for it to keep in contact with sensible experience; to maintain its own vitality it needs a great expanse in which to breathe and unceasing exchanges.

But the State, with all its profane culture, is in the Church, as the earth is in the firmament. The laity are in the Church; the more laic it becomes, the more boldly it advances to the most exposed frontiers, the more must the perennial philosophy, to preserve its integrity, remain in continuity with the superhuman sources without which human things fail, with the sacred wisdom which transcends it and whose native country is the contemplative activity of the Church. It was therefore in the nature of things and in conformity with the eternal order that before seeking its fortune in the wide world it should first have been commissioned by the papacy.

The particular favour shown by the Church, the recommendations and exhortations of the Popes, are not and make no pretence of being an intrinsic demonstration of the truth of Thomism. They are merely extrinsic arguments and guarantees, indications determining the mind of the believer to a well-founded confidence. Unbelievers, no doubt, are unmoved by them; nay more, recommendations of the sort incline them rather to suspect a philosophy under such patronage. The Church does not, therefore, speak in bated breath; she is not in the least anxious to make a compromise between philosophers and herself and Jesus Christ; she doubtless considers that if such unbelievers refuse to listen to primary Truth, they will be still more reluctant to listen to metaphysical arguments because their minds are prejudiced; if they profess to be scandalized at seeing a science honoured by faith, she regards their scandal as pharisaical. In any event it would be ridiculous to parade before them her feeling in favour of any one philosophy.

As for believers, they are well aware that no philosophy can be imposed upon them as a dogma. But if the philosophy of St. Thomas is not therefore endowed in their eyes, by the mere fact of being recommended by the Church, with the supra-rational value of an article of faith—or in the special province of rational disciplines with that evidence compelling adhesion which a philosophy either possesses in itself or never will possess—nevertheless among extrinsic indications likely to produce a true opinion, capable of inclining a mind in good faith first to place its trust in a doctrine, then to examine it, to study it for itself with respect and confidence, or rather with that joy which the reasonable hope of encountering the truth inspires, they can find none more persuasive and significant than such testimonies.

In the special province of science, the argument from authority is the weakest of all.[1] But in the province of apprenticeship, in the order of preparation for the reception of knowledge, in the *via ad scientiam,* in which it is precisely with the support of extrinsic indications and arguments that the mind gradually becomes accustomed to make progress for itself by steps of evidence, the authority of a master does in fact play a preponderating part. For we are not mathematical angels, established by the natural light of our reason in a virtual scientific state which we need only expand by discourse, we are, alas! children of men learning in order to know, and knowing, learning again. Many misconceptions of the

[1] St. Thomas Aquinas, *Sum. Theol.,* I, 1, 8, *ad* 2.

attitude of the Church with regard to the philosophy of St. Thomas would spontaneously disappear, if it were realised that it is in the first place a question of pedagogy and education: even the preposterous [2] current derivation from *educere* will serve to make a scholastic point; let it be said that it is a question of "educing" philosophical knowledge, of bringing it into existence out of the potentiality of a mind which is at first a mere *tabula rasa.*

In this spirit and in order that it may be more precisely understood how a philosophy, which, in itself, depends solely on evidence and reason, could nevertheless receive the recommendation of the Church with a unique and extraordinarily significant insistence, I would offer the following observations. They will, I trust, be sufficient to prove that it is equally false either to accuse the Catholic Church of imposing an "ideological conformity" upon the faithful in the matter of philosophy or to imagine that a Catholic may regard the philosophy of St. Thomas as something to which he may be

[2] [Preposterous, because the word is originally an agricultural metaphor and means "to grow a crop," as in Catullus (xii, 41: *"quem [florem] mulcent aurae, firmat sol, educat imber."* Cf. the observations of the late Professor Burnet in his Romanes lecture at Oxford (1923) on *Ignorance,* p. 10. The word *seminary* exactly defines the essence of education. "As to Education," says Cobbett in his *Advice to Young Men* (Oxford, 1906, p. 39), "this word is now applied exclusively to things which are taught in schools; but education means rearing up, and the French speak of the education of pigs and sheep." Tr.]

"indifferent," as a philosophy proposing itself for his consideration in the same way and in the same conditions as any other philosophical system.

In this short statement—in which, as I indicated in the beginning, I propose simply to consider St. Thomas as a philosopher, leaving the theologian out of account—my only desire is to put the reader face to face with the official statements of the Supreme Pontiffs which have not in every case secured the amount of public attention they deserve. We shall therefore consider in the first place, from the point of view of actual fact, historically and textually, what the attitude of the Popes has been in practice with regard to St. Thomas.

Nevertheless, to light us on the way, an attempt should first be made, by way of introduction, to obtain a summary, but none the less exact, idea of the general truths which dominate the whole discussion, that is to say the rôle and authority of the Church in matters of philosophy.

On this point certain elementary truths logically compel the assent of every man who admits a revelation by God proposed by the Church of Christ, elementary truths which the Church herself has been careful to embody in dogmatic definitions.[3]

[3] Cf. Denzinger-Bannwart, *Encheiridion Symbolorum* (16th and 17th editions, Freiburg, 1928), §§ 1674, 1681–1684, 1714, 1786, 1797–1799, and Vacant's *Études théologiques sur le Concile du Vatican*, I, p. 347; St.

They are here recalled for the sake of clarity.

One truth cannot contradict another, for that would be to destroy the very first principle of reason; and the theory of double truth, invented in the Middle Ages by the Averroists and taken up again in our day by a few modernists—according to which the same thing can be true in faith and false in reason or *vice versa*—is sheer absurdity. "Although faith is above reason," the Vatican Council declares, "yet there can be no genuine disagreement between faith and reason: for it is the same God Who, on the one hand, reveals the mysteries and inspires souls with faith and, on the other, has endowed the human mind with the light of reason, and God cannot possibly deny His own nature or one truth ever contradict another. The vain appearance of such contradiction occasionally arises from the fact that the dogmas of faith are not understood and expounded in the sense in which they are understood by the Church or that erroneous opinions are taken for statements of reason."

The necessary consequences are these.

Philosophy, like every science, is independent of revelation and faith in its own peculiar sphere and principles and, taking them for its starting-point, develops autonomously with the natural light of

Thomas Aquinas, *Sum. Theol.*, I, i, 1; *Sum. contra Gent.*, I, 4; and Garrigou-Lagrange, *De Revelatione*, I, pp. 411–415.

reason for its own peculiar light and evidence for sole criterion;

Philosophy is nevertheless subject to the magistracy of faith, every proposition made by a philosopher destructive of a revealed truth being manifestly erroneous, and reason enlightened by faith being alone competent to judge whether any particular proposition by a philosopher—that is, a man employing more or less correctly unaided natural reason—is as a matter of fact contrary or not to faith.

Revelation thus plays the part of norm or negative rule in regard to philosophy, that is to say that, without encroaching on its principles or intervening in its methods or its own peculiar activity, it has a right to check the conclusions of philosophy.

It is clear that, once the fact of revelation is admitted, philosophy can suffer no harm from any such indirect subordination to faith. Like art and every other human discipline, it is free and mistress in its own sphere, but that sphere is limited and subordinate; it does not therefore enjoy an absolute freedom, but is there anybody absolutely free but God Himself? To be limited in its freedom to make a mistake, to have an exterior check, a railing, as it were, against error, is in reality a great benefit for philosophy. For, if it is true, as Cicero says, that there is no folly in the world but has found some philosopher to support it—which comes to saying with Holy Writ that there is no end to the number of fools, even among philosophers—then it must be admitted that philosophy, if it is to perform successfully the work of reason, must require—I do not say in itself, I say in man—the assistance it receives from the control of revelation which saves it from committing many regrettable errors.

The better to appreciate the importance and even in a sense the necessity of such a benefit, we should bear in mind the common teaching of theologians, confirmed by the Vatican Council, that the natural weakness of man is so great that the human reason is incapable, without some special help from God, of attaining to the possession of the great truths of the natural order as a whole (*collective*) and without admixture of error, although each, considered separately, is within its range. We then realize that over and above the essential function of negative norm or external check before referred to, faith has also a positive office to fulfil in regard to the philosophical reason, that is to indicate the goal and direct the mind, *veluti stella rectrix,* like a guiding star.

Lastly, philosophy may be considered no longer in itself and in its own peculiar sphere, but as part and parcel of the contexture of a more exalted science: theology, the science of revealed truths, which we possess, according to St. Thomas, by way of participation in the science peculiar to God and His Saints. Theology cannot develop in the human mind without making use of the philosophical truths, which are established by reason and which it puts in contact with the data of faith to produce out of those data the consequences they virtually contain. It so superelevates philosophy and makes use of it then as an instrument. It is immediately apparent that these living bonds provide yet another reason confirming the subordination of philosophy to the magistracy of revelation and faith; it is for theology, in itself independent of every philosophical system, to judge the propositions advanced by philosophers in its own light, and of the various philosophical systems to adopt the one most capable of being in its hands the best instrument of truth.

Such are the elementary notions that logically compel the assent of the mind, once the fact of Catholic Revelation is posited.

What follows? It follows that those who have received the grace of faith cannot philosophize in utter disregard of that faith, *stella rectrix,* and of theology, by devising a system of water-tight compartments. Their philosophy remains rigorously distinct from their faith and admits only the rational in its peculiar structure. But it cannot be divorced from faith; and it is clear that the natural impulse of every believer is to reject as false philosophical opinions which he perceives to be contrary to revealed truth. Every man is morally bound to defend his property and the property of God against error.

But will the Church in this case abandon every one to his own unaided resources? If she did so, she would fail in the mission imposed upon her to preserve the deposit of faith and her duty to protect souls. She will therefore intervene, and when she is confronted with a philosophical error she considers sufficiently grave (whether that error directly destroy a revealed truth or a truth merely connected with the deposit of revelation) she will condemn it; she will also recommend positively the philosophical doctrine she considers most capable of confirming and strengthening the mind in relation to faith; she will exercise her sacred magistracy, therefore, in the sphere of philosophy.

In speaking of the Church—I beg to be excused this parenthesis—let us think of her as she really is. Do not let us entertain any attenuated conception of her nature; do not let us think of a mere spiritual administration: let us remember that she herself is a mystery; that she is the mystical body of Christ, a living person, both human and divine, whose head is Christ and all of whose members are united by the Holy Ghost; the great Contemplative whose ardent desire is to beget all men unto eternal life, and whose movements, executed no doubt by human instruments, proceed from the divine wisdom and the most pure gifts of grace. We shall not then bargain upon the terms of our allegiance, we shall not follow her like fractious children who have to be dragged along; we shall understand that her doctrinal authority is not confined to solemn definitions of what cannot be denied without lapsing into heresy, but extends, on the contrary, according to every degree and inflection in the tone of voice and the authoritativeness of the statement made by what is described as the ordinary magistracy of the Church, to everything affecting the integrity of faith in souls.

From the principles just laid down, a final conclusion emerges. When the Church exercises her authority in the philosophical sphere, she does so essentially in relation to faith, in relation to revealed truth, the deposit of which it is her duty to guard. But since faith presupposes reason as grace presupposes nature, in order perfectly to discharge her function as guardian of the faith the Church is also, and secondarily, appointed by God to be the guardian of the health of the reason, guardian of the natural order, as of the natural law. Let us say therefore that she has a double task to perform: to safeguard the deposit of revelation and, secondarily, to safeguard the natural rectitude of reason itself. And it is in virtue of this double duty that in exercising her authority in the philosophical sphere, she works in fact for the greater good of reason. The Church is not for the world, said St. Augustine; and yet she acts as though she were there for the good of the world.

It is common knowledge that the great doctrinal synthesis effected by St. Thomas in the thirteenth century appeared to the eyes of contemporaries a hazardous innovation. Why? Because St. Thomas, following his master Albert the Great, had adopted the philosophy of Aristotle in order to transform it into the service of the faith, and because Aristotle, who had but recently reached the Christian world through the compromising intermediary of Arab translators and commentators, had a very bad reputation. Certain members of the old school were so startled that, a few years after the death of St. Thomas, in spite of the enormous influence his philosophy had already acquired, some of the theses he professed were censured by the bishop of Paris, Étienne Tempier, and two English bishops. Étienne Tempier, however, was not the Church. As for the novelty of St. Thomas, it did not derive from the fact that he changed or altered the theological speculation which had been inherited from the Fathers and elaborated in the schools of the Middle Ages; it derived on the contrary from the fact that he carried it to its point of scientific perfection, making use for that purpose as an instrument, but not without elevating and purifying it, of the most vigorously rational, the most highly developed, the most analytical philosophy that the Greek genius could ever conceive.

Now it is a very remarkable thing that from the very beginning the Popes not only encouraged St. Thomas in his work,[4] but also discerned in the Thomist synthesis an incomparable value and quality, and considered that in it the whole Christian tradition had borne fruit. John XXII, who canonized Friar Thomas Aquinas in 1323, fifty years after his death, declared that his doctrine could have proceeded only from some miraculous intervention by God, *"doctrina ejus non potuit esse sine miraculo,"* and that he alone did more to enlighten the Church than all the other doctors together. Twenty years later, on the 6th February, 1344, Clement VI testified to the spread of the philosophy of St. Thomas in the universal Church, and in 1346 enjoined on the Dominican Order to adhere steadfastly to it. The Dominicans, who had already in their general

---

[4] "Even during the lifetime of the Saint, Alexander IV had no hesitation in addressing him in these terms: 'To Our beloved Son, Thomas Aquinas, distinguished alike for nobility of blood and integrity of character, who has acquired by the grace of God the treasure of divine and human learning.'" Pius XI, Encyclical *Studiorum Ducem.*

Chapters in 1279 and 1286 chosen Thomas Aquinas for their Doctor, were thus commissioned by the Pope to preserve and maintain his teaching intact and the teaching itself was officially proposed, under the ægis of the Angelic Doctor, for the protection of the Catholic mind.

Urban V in 1368 ordered the University of Toulouse "to follow the doctrine of the blessed Thomas as being truthful and Catholic and to exert itself to the utmost to develop it." There would be no end, were it given in detail, to the witness of the Supreme Pontiffs: Nicholas V; Pius IV; St. Pius V, who proclaimed Thomas Aquinas a doctor of the Church; Sixtus V; Clement VIII; Paul V; Alexander VII; Innocent XI; Innocent XII; Benedict XIII; Clement XII; Benedict XIV. . . . Let it suffice to recall Innocent VI's observation that "those who have a firm grasp of the philosophy of St. Thomas are never found far astray from the path of truth, and whoever has opposed it has always been suspect of error," and to observe that in the stout volume [5] devoted by Père Berthier to *St. Thomas Aquinas, the Common Doctor of the Church*, the testimonies of the Popes occupy no less than 250 octavo pages. Ever since the Council of Lyons, held in 1274, the very year of the death of

---

[5] J. J. Berthier, *Sanctus Thomas Aquinas Doctor Communis Ecclesiae*, vol. I. *Testimonia Ecclesiae*, Romae, 1914.

163

St. Thomas (he died at Fossanova on his way to the Council, but his philosophy was present there and the Council borrowed from it the forms of judgment in which it condemned the errors of the Greeks) and the Council of Vienne (1311–1312), at which the Church defined the substantial unity of the human being in the very words of St. Thomas, it may be confidently asserted that the Fathers of all the Councils have had recourse to the intellectual weapons prepared by him and have always shown themselves absolutely faithful to his principles. This is nowhere more apparent than in the definitions of the Council of Trent. "For ever since the happy death of the saintly Doctor," wrote Pius X, "the Church has not held a single Council but he has been present at it with the wealth of his doctrine." [6] If however, not even such a Doctor was exempt from the taint of human limitations, where the divine mysteries are concerned, in this respect that the privilege of the Immaculate Conception, much controverted at his time, was not formally taught by him (it was even bitterly opposed for some centuries by part of his school), it must be observed that the reserve maintained by him in this particular was determined by his adherence (from theological prudence and in order not to anticipate

---

[6] Motu proprio *Doctoris Angelici*, 29th June, 1914. The words are adopted by Pius XI in the Encyclical *Studiorum Ducem*.

the judgment of the Roman Church) to the implicit without venturing so far as any precise definition; such caution discloses not the slightest defect in his principles, which, in reality, by ensuring the proper course like a "helm," [7] prepared the way no

[7] "The Franciscan school, at the instigation of Scotus and with the enthusiastic support of the faithful, asserted with all its strength that the Mother of God ought to be and was in fact immaculate. They were determined to take any course to reach that port which their ardent love for the Most Holy Virgin made them eager to attain: and they were therefore more concerned to speed up the ship and quicken the journey than to plot the exact course.

"St. Thomas and his school, accustomed to apply the brake of reason to mere emotion and—changing the metaphor—not to hazard an advance over the mysterious sea of dogma, without light from the beacons of dogmas already defined, asserted no less strenuously that the Mother of God, like every child of Adam, must have been really and personally redeemed by the Blood of Calvary, and that they were prepared to block the way of the Mother of God even, so long as they considered that she had not progressed far forward on the path of the personal *debitum*, the only one motivating redemption by the blood of Jesus Christ.

"Exposed to this dual influence—the fervour of the Scotists and the Thomist helm—the barque of the Immaculate made slow but none the less steady progress for centuries. Without Scotus and his School it would never have moved at all, or at any rate would have made but little progress; without the intervention of St. Thomas and his disciples it would certainly have lost its way. After God and His Church, it is to Scotus and his School that we are indebted for the definition of the Immaculate Conception, but it is to St. Thomas and his disciples that we are indebted for the definition of the true Immaculate Conception." F. Marín-Sola, *L'Évolution homogène du dogme catholique*, Freiburg, 1924, vol. I, pp. 327–328.

Cf. on this question, above all, Père del Prado's *Divus Thomas et Bulla Dogmatica "Ineffabilis Deus,"* Freiburg, 1919. The teaching of St. Thomas (against certain erroneous arguments on behalf of the Immaculate Conception) is that the Mother of the Saviour also has been redeemed by the merits of her Son and that she must be acknowledged to possess all degrees of purity, provided they be compatible with her redemption by Jesus Christ. All that is then required is a more explicit statement, with the addition that her redemption was a preserving redemption (presupposing not sin but the *debitum*, the personal and proximate debt remitted by the anticipated merits of Christ at the very moment of the creation and infusion of her soul) to have the idea of the Immaculate Conception as the Church has defined it and as it is very exactly expressed in the prayer of less than the fervour of Scotus and the Franciscan school for the dogmatic definition promulgated in 1854 by Pius IX.

But to come down to the last quarter of the nineteenth century. The matter then assumed a new aspect. St. Thomas no longer appeared as merely the master of sacred learning, whose philosophy presided over the solemn acts of the ecclesiastical magistracy and constituted the theological reserve of the Church. The Pope then addressed himself to the human reason and summoned it to return to the Angelic Doctor, to ask him the way of enlightenment, and, after its long experience of so many negations, intoxications and revulsions, to restore the great affirmations of Thomist philosophy. On the 4th August, 1879, Leo XIII published the Encyclical *Aeterni Patris* [8] from which the renaissance of scholastic studies dates its origin. Everyone will find it profitable to read (or re-read) that Encyclical from end to end, for it contains a defence and apology on behalf of philosophy, its value as a science, its dignity and utility among men and in Christian society, which, proceeding from the Vicar of Christ addressing the universe, are invested with a singular gravity and nobility. After a brief summary of the

the feast of the 8th December: *"Deus . . . qui ex morte ejusdem Filii tui praevisa, eam ab omni labe praeservasti . . ."*

[8] The text of this Encyclical will be found in translation in the Appendix, p. 189.

history of philosophy throughout the Christian centuries, in the age of the Fathers and the great Schoolmen, the Pope says:

"Above all the Doctors of the Schools towers the figure of Thomas Aquinas, the leader and master of them all, who, as Cajetan observes, 'because he had the utmost reverence for the holy Doctors of antiquity seems to have inherited in a way the intellect of all, *intellectum omnium quodammodo sortitus est.*' [9] Thomas gathered their doctrines together—they had long lain dispersed like the scattered limbs as it were of a body—and knitted them into one whole. He disposed them in marvellous order and increased them to such an extent that he is rightly and deservedly considered the preeminent guardian and glory of the Catholic Church."

Leo XIII then proceeds to lay remarkable stress on the capital importance of a Thomist renaissance not only in regard to religious truth and the protection of consecrated property in souls but also in regard to profane culture and the whole movement of art and science. The arts indeed,

"have habitual recourse to philosophy as to controlling wisdom for their supreme regulation and proper method and derive from philosophy as from a common source of life the spirit animating them."

[9] In II–II, 148, 4, *in finem.*

167

As for the natural sciences,

"supreme insult is offered and supreme injury done to [the scholastic philosophy] by the allegation that it is opposed to the progress and development of such sciences. [On the contrary] as the Schoolmen, therein following the common tradition of the holy Fathers, taught at every step in anthropology that the mind cannot raise itself except by sensible things to the knowledge of incorporeal and immaterial things, so they also realized that nothing could be more useful to the philosopher than the diligent scrutiny of the secrets of nature and the devotion of much time and care to the study of physical phenomena. . . . The natural sciences themselves, which are held in such high estimation at the present day, and everywhere attract through so many magnificent discoveries an admiration without parallel, so far from suffering the least harm, would, on the contrary, derive singular advantage from a restoration of the ancient philosophy. . . . For the mere consideration of facts and the observation of nature are not sufficient . . . the scientist must rise to a higher plane. . . . Scholastic philosophy, wisely taught, would contribute to such investigations a marvellous increase of energy and a flood of illumination. [And the Pope concludes:] We earnestly exhort you for the protection and glory of the Catholic faith, for the welfare of society, for the advancement of all sciences, to restore the precious wisdom of St. Thomas and to propagate it as far as possible."

We are now witnessing a great intellectual movement launched by the will and with the expressed encouragement of the watchmen on the top of the towers of the Church; that is one of the best examples of what may be described as the *medicinal* action of the papacy on wounded humanity.

The acts in which Leo XIII confirmed and further defined the exhortations contained in the Encyclical *Aeterni Patris* are innumerable. The defence of the faith, "the advancement of science, the salvation of society are at stake." [10] In his addresses to the universal Church, to Redemptorists, Franciscans, Dominicans, Benedictines, to bishops, universities and seminaries, throughout twenty-five years, in encyclicals, briefs, letters and audiences, he unceasingly recommended a return to St. Thomas and couched his recommendations, as often as the occasion presented itself, in words as precise as they were imperative:

"Those who are desirous of becoming true philosophers—and religious especially ought to be animated by such a desire—are bound [he told the Friars Minor [11]] to establish the principles and foundations of their philosophy on St. Thomas Aquinas."

"If there are doctors to be found who disagree with St. Thomas [he wrote to the Jesuits [12]], how-

[10] Letter of the 12th December, 1884, to M. Pidal.
[11] Letter of the 25th November, 1898.
[12] Letter of the 30th December, 1892.

ever great their merits may be in other respects, hesitation is not permissible. The former must be sacrificed to the latter."

On the 18th January, 1880, he ordered the Dominicans to publish, at the expense of the Holy See, a monumental edition of St. Thomas; on the 4th August, of the same year, he placed "all Catholic universities, colleges, faculties and schools" under the patronage of St. Thomas; and in the Brief published on that occasion he expressed his conviction that "the Thomist philosophy pre-eminently possesses singular power and energy to cure the ills afflicting our time."

"The philosophy of St. Thomas [he went on to say] is so far ranging that it contains, like a sea, all the wisdom which has been transmitted from antiquity. Not only was St. Thomas fully acquainted with every true statement made, every problem prudently resolved, by pagan philosophers, the Fathers and Doctors of the Church, and his own distinguished predecessors, but he has also increased, perfected and ordered the whole with such a perspicacious appreciation of essential principles, such perfection of method and propriety of expression that he seems to have bequeathed to his successors only the possibility of imitating him, having deprived them of the possibility of rivalling them.

"And this consideration also is not without importance: his philosophy, being informed and as it were armed with principles of great breadth of application, answers the needs not of an age only but of all time, and is admirably fitted to refute ceaselessly recurrent errors."

Leo XIII himself, "to prove the 'actuality' of this philosophy and its relation to the problems of the day, makes use of it continually in the teaching of the Church." [13] He encouraged and supported in every way institutions and enterprises intended to spread it, more particularly the work undertaken, not without strenuous opposition, by the prelate who was later to become Cardinal Mercier.

Finally, in his encyclical letter of the 8th September, 1899, to the French clergy, he laid renewed emphasis upon the matter, and once more opposed St. Thomas to Kantian subjectivism, which he denounced as the danger *par excellence*:

"We said in Our Encyclical *Aeterni Patris,* which We once more recommend your seminarists and their teachers carefully to peruse and We based Ourselves upon the authority of St. Paul to say so that it is by the idle subtleties of bad philosophy, *per philosophiam et inanem fallaciam (Coll.* ii, 8), that the faithful suffer their minds as a rule to be cheated and the purity of the faith becomes corrupted among men. We added—and the events of

---

[13] Cf. Père Janvier's *Action intellect. et polit. de Léon XIII en France* and, more generally, all the Encyclicals of Leo XIII, particularly *Rerum novarum.*

the last twenty years have very sadly confirmed the reflections and apprehensions. We then expressed—'Anyone considering the critical state of the times in which we live, and reflecting upon the condition of public and domestic affairs, will easily perceive that a fruitful cause of the evils that actually oppress us and others which we may reasonably apprehend is to be found in the fact that erroneous theories respecting our duty to God and our responsibilities as men, originally propounded in philosophical schools, have gradually permeated all ranks of society and secured acceptance among the majority of men.'

"We condemn such doctrines again as being only nominally philosophical, and as conducing logically to universal scepticism and irreligion, by shaking the very foundations of human knowledge. We are profoundly grieved to learn that for some years past Catholics have thought it possible to follow such a philosophy as under the specious pretext of emancipating the human mind from every preconceived idea and all illusion denies it the right to make any affirmation beyond its own activities, so sacrificing to a radical subjectivism all the certitudes which the traditional metaphysics, sanctioned by the authority of the most vigorous minds, laid down as the essential and unshaken foundations for the demonstration of the existence of God, the spirituality and immortality of the soul, and the objective reality of the exterior world."

Let it be observed that about the same time Rudolf Eucken, on the Protestant side, was also contrasting St. Thomas and Kant as two worlds in irreducible opposition.[14]

There is still more to come. Pius X, Benedict XV and Pius XI have continued and confirmed in every way the intellectual work of Leo XIII. It is more than ever important to have the actual texts before our eyes. This passage especially from the Encyclical *Pascendi* of the 8th September, 1907, should be borne in mind:

"In the first place, with regard to studies, it is Our will, and We hereby explicitly ordain, that the Scholastic philosophy be considered as the foundation of sacred studies. It goes without saying that 'if there be any proposition too subtly investigated or too inconsiderately taught by the Doctors of the School, any tenet of theirs not strictly in conformity with subsequent discoveries or in any way improbable in itself, it is no part of Our intention to propose that for the imitation of Our age.[15] What is of capital importance, however, is that in prescribing that the scholastic philosophy is to be followed, We have in mind particularly the philosophy which has been transmitted to us by St. Thomas Aquinas. We therefore declare that all the orders issued in this regard by Our Predecessor remain in full force and where need be We renew and confirm them and order them to be strictly observed by all concerned. Let Bishops urge

[14] *"Thomas von Aquino und Kant, ein Kampf zweier Welten,"* Kant-studien, vol. VI, 1901.
[15] Leo XIII, Encyclical *Aeterni Patris.*

and compel their observance in future in any seminary in which they may have been neglected. The same injunction applies also to Superiors of religious orders. And we warn teachers to bear in mind that to deviate from St. Thomas, in metaphysics especially, is to run very considerable risk."

In his Motu Proprio *Sacrorum Antistitum* of the 1st September, 1910, addressed to all Bishops and Superiors-General of religious Orders charged with the duty of supervising the education of aspirants to the priesthood, Pius X reiterated his instructions:

"So far as studies are concerned, it is Our will, and We hereby explicitly ordain, that the Scholastic philosophy be considered the basis of sacred studies. . . . And in prescribing that the Scholastic philosophy be followed, we have in mind particularly—this is of capital importance—the philosophy that has been transmitted to us by St. Thomas Aquinas."

"Particularly" was the word used by the Pope.

On the 29th June, 1914, in the Motu Proprio *Doctoris Angelici* [16] which gathers together and summarizes all the pontifical teaching on St. Thomas, and powerfully testifies to the indivisibility of his doctrine, the Pope continued:

"Now because the word We used in the text of that letter, recommending the philosophy of Aqui-

[16] Cf. the text of this Motu Proprio in the Appendix, p. 215.

174

nas, was 'particularly' and not 'exclusively,' certain persons persuaded themselves that they were acting in conformity to Our Will or at any rate not actively opposing it in adopting indiscriminately and adhering to the philosophical opinions of any other Doctor of the School, even though such opinions were contrary to the principles of St. Thomas. They were greatly deceived. In recommending St. Thomas to Our subjects as supreme guide in the Scholastic philosophy, it goes without saying that Our intention was to be understood as referring to those principles above all upon which that philosophy is based as its foundation. For just as the opinion of certain ancients is to be rejected which maintains that it makes no difference to the truth of the Faith what any man thinks about the nature of creation, provided his opinions on the nature of God be sound, because error concerning the nature of creation begets a false knowledge of God, so the principles of philosophy laid down by St. Thomas Aquinas are to be religiously and inviolably observed, because they are the means of acquiring such a knowledge of creation as is most congruent with the Faith (*Contra Gent.*, II, ii and iii); of refuting all the errors of all the ages, and of enabling man to distinguish clearly what things are to be attributed to God and to God alone (*Ibid., iii; Sum. Theol.*, I, 12, 4; 54. 1). They also marvellously illustrate the diversity and analogy between God and His works. . . .

". . . St. Thomas perfected and augmented still further by the almost angelic quality of his intel-

175

lect all this superb patrimony of wisdom which he inherited from his predecessors and applied it to prepare, illustrate and protect sacred doctrine in the minds of men (*In librum Boethii 'De Trinitate,'* q. 2, a. 3). Sound reason suggests that it would be folly to neglect it and religion will not suffer it to be in any way attenuated. And rightly, because, if Catholic doctrine is once deprived of this strong bulwark, it is useless to seek the slightest assistance for its defence in a philosophy whose principles are either common to the errors of materialism, monism, pantheism, socialism and modernism or certainly not opposed to such systems. The reason is that the capital theses in the philosophy of St. Thomas are not to be placed in the category of opinions capable of being debated one way or another, but are to be considered as the foundations upon which the whole science of natural and divine things is based; if such principles are once removed or in any way impaired, it must necessarily follow that students of the sacred sciences will ultimately fail to perceive so much as the meaning of the words in which the dogmas of divine revelation are proposed by the magistracy of the Church.

"We therefore desired that all teachers of philosophy and sacred theology should be warned that if they deviated so much as a step, in metaphysics especially, from Aquinas, they exposed themselves to grave risk. We now go further, and solemnly declare that those who in their interpretation misrepresent or affect to despise the principles and major theses (*principia et pronuntiata majora*) of

176

his philosophy are not only not following St. Thomas but are even far astray from the holy Doctor. If the doctrine of any writer or saint has ever been approved by Us or Our Predecessors with such singular commendation and in such a way that to the commendation were added an invitation and order to propagate and defend it, it may easily be understood that it was commended to the extent that it agreed with the principles of Aquinas or was in no way opposed to them."

All that thereafter remained to be done was to prescribe to teachers directly under the authority of the Church the teaching of the philosophy of St. Thomas, and that by a law inscribed in the actual code of the decrees of the Church. This was done; and such an enactment surpasses everything hitherto done by the Popes. In the new Code of Canon Law promulgated by Benedict XV, teachers in Catholic schools are ordered:

"to deal in every particular with the studies of mental philosophy and theology and the education of pupils in such sciences according to the method, doctrine and principles of the Angelic Doctor and religiously to adhere thereto." [17]

Thomas Aquinas, therefore, is no longer proposed

[17] Cf. Canon 1366, § 2.—To preserve the peculiar customs and traditions of the Eastern Church, the first canon in the Code of Canon Law lays down that the Code applies only to the Latin Church. The juridical obligation to make St. Thomas the basis of studies does not therefore affect, by the letter of the Code, the Eastern Church. But what is of most importance here to consider is the intention and desire of the Church which find ex-

to us as merely one doctor of eminence among others. He is the Doctor *par excellence* and occupies an entirely unique place. He realizes in its fulness the title of *Doctor communis Ecclesiae* which was formerly given to him. So far as a philosopher is distinguished to an exceptionally eminent degree by the characteristics of a certain spiritual community, Descartes, Malebranche and Auguste Comte may be said to be specifically French philosophers, Fichte and Hegel specifically German philosophers. St. Thomas, on the other hand, is the specifically Catholic Doctor, the philosopher and theologian of Peter and Catholicity.

Pope Benedict XV wrote later—and his is one of the highest commendations yet bestowed on St. Thomas—that "the Church has declared the philosophy of Thomas Aquinas to be her own special philosophy, *cum Thomae doctrinam Ecclesia suam propriam edixit esse.*" [18] He was followed by Pope Pius XI in his Apostolic Letter of the 1st August,

pression adapted to time and place in her laws. There can be no doubt that in the mind of the Church it is in the light of the principles of St. Thomas that the wisdom of the Greek Fathers and the traditions of the East are also to be understood and systematized. The teaching and exhortations of the Popes on this subject are of absolutely universal import.

[18] Encyclical *Fausto appetente die* for the seventh centenary of the death of St. Dominic (29th June, 1924). Cf. also the testimony given to St. Thomas, whose philosophy is "according to Christ," in the Motu Proprio *Non Multo* on the Roman Academy of St. Thomas (31st December, 1914): "We therefore, in the conviction common also to Our Predecessors that We need concern Ourselves only with that philosophy which is according to Christ (*Col.* ii, 8) and that consequently We are bound to insist on a philosophy according to the principles and method of Aquinas. . . ."

· 1922, *Officiorum omnium*, on the education of the clergy:

"Once the programme of literary studies has been completed, Our seminarians shall diligently spend at least two years' study in philosophy so that they may be adequately prepared for the course of sacred theology. We mean by philosophy the Scholastic philosophy diligently elaborated by the labours of the holy Fathers and the Doctors of the School and brought to its highest degree of perfection by the industry and genius of Thomas Aquinas, that philosophy which Our illustrious Predecessor Leo XIII had no hesitation in describing as 'the bulwark of the Faith and strong rampart of Religion' (Encyclical Letter *Aeterni Patris*). It is indeed the great glory of Leo that he restored the Christian philosophy and rekindled love and devotion for the Angelic Doctor; and it is Our considered opinion that of all the valuable services he rendered Church and State in his long pontificate this was so important that, in default of the rest, it alone would have secured immortality to that great Pontiff.

"Let teachers of philosophy therefore, in lecturing to seminarians on this science, be careful to follow not only the system or method of St. Thomas, but also his doctrine and principles, and the more zealously because they must know that no Doctor of the Church is so much feared and dreaded by modernists and other enemies of the Catholic Faith as Aquinas.

179

"Our observations concerning philosophy apply also to the teaching of sacred theology. For, as Pope Sixtus V says, 'This very salutary branch of learning derives its principles from Holy Scripture, the acts of the Popes, the works of the Fathers and the decrees of the Councils; the knowledge and practical application of theology have always been of powerful assistance to the Church in enabling her to understand exactly and interpret faithfully the text of Scripture, to read and expound the Fathers with greater certainty and profit, to detect and refute errors and heresies. But it is above all in times such as the present, when we are living amidst the dangers described by the Apostle, and blasphemous men, exultant and seductive, unceasingly progress in evil, themselves steeped in error leading others astray, that it is of sovereign necessity for confirming the dogmas of the Catholic Faith and the refutation of heresies' (Bull *Triumphantis*, 1588).

"Now what gives theology the force of a genuine science, capable of providing, in the admirable words of Our lamented Predecessor Pope Benedict XV (Motu Proprio *De Romana Sancti Thomæ Academia*, 1914) as complete an explanation as human reason allows and an invincible defence of the truth of divine revelation is nothing other than the Scholastic philosophy employed in the service, under the guidance and leadership of Aquinas, of theology. It is the Scholastic philosophy which provides 'that exact and interrelated coherence between things and their causes, that order and disposition as of soldiers drawn-up in battle array, those perspicuous definitions and distinctions, that strength in argument and subtlety in controversy, whereby light is distinguished from darkness and truth from error. . . .' (Sixtus V, *loc. cit.*).

"The consequence is that they ill conceive their duty in the education of youth who neglect the Scholastic method and consider that all theological instruction should be given according to what is known as the 'positive method'; and those teachers fail still more in their duty whose method of teaching theology is merely to give learned disquisitions on a chronological table of dogmas and heresies. A positive method is the necessary complement to the Scholastic method, but by itself alone is far from sufficient. Our seminarians must be educated not only to demonstrate the truth of the Faith but also to illustrate and defend it; now to pass in review the dogmas of the Faith and opposing errors in chronological order, is to teach ecclesiastical history, not theology."

Finally, the Encyclical *Studiorum Ducem,* by setting out clearly the combination of sanctity and doctrine in the Angelic Doctor and showing the union in him, along with the grace of the eloquence of wisdom, "of both forms of wisdom, the acquired and the infused," places as it were before our eyes the treasure of love, of holy apostolic energy and ever-living virtuality in the philosophy of St.

181

Thomas, and insists also on the *catholicity* of that philosophy. Adopting the important expression of Benedict XV, it gives an official consecration to the oldest, as it is also undoubtedly the finest, of the titles of St. Thomas:

"We so heartily approve the magnificent tribute of praise bestowed upon this most divine genius that We consider that St. Thomas should be called not only the Angelic, but also the Common or Universal Doctor of the Church: for the Church has adopted his philosophy for her own as innumerable documents of every kind attest." [19]

At the same time this Encyclical, by dwelling upon, and giving the sanction of authority to, certain elements in the teaching of St. Thomas, offers us some notable and definite reasons for the adoption by the Church of that philosophy.

"But as he was accustomed [writes Pius XI] to contemplate all things in God, the first Cause and ultimate End of all things, as it was easy for him to follow in his *Summa Theologica* no less than in his life the two kinds of wisdom before referred to. He himself describes them as follows: 'The wisdom which is acquired by human effort . . . gives

[19] Encyclical *Studiorum Ducem* of the 29th June, 1923. The text will be found in the Appendix, pp. 221–240. Cf. also Père Benoît Lavaud's commentary in *Saint Thomas, Guide des Études*, Paris, Téqui, 1925.

a man a sound judgment with regard to divine things according as he makes a perfect use of reason. . . . But there is another kind of wisdom which comes down from above . . . and judges divine things in virtue of a certain connaturality with them. This wisdom is the gift of the Holy Ghost . . . and through it a man becomes perfect in divine things, not only by learning but also by experiencing divine things' (II–II, 45, 1).

"This wisdom, therefore, which comes down from, or is infused by, God, accompanied by the other gifts of the Holy Ghost, continually grew and increased in St. Thomas, along with charity, the mistress and queen of all the virtues. Indeed it was an absolutely certain doctrine of his that the love of God should ever continually increase 'in accordance with the very words of the commandment: *Thou shalt love the Lord thy God, with thy whole heart* . . . for the whole and the perfect are one same thing. . . . Now the end of the commandment, as the Apostle says (*I Tim.* i, 5), is charity; but no standard of measure is applicable to the end, only to such means as conduce to the end' (II–II, 184, 3). This is the very reason why the perfection of charity falls under the commandment as the end to which we ought all to strive, each according to his degree."

Two important theses of the Common Doctor are thus affirmed, one drawing a distinction between the wisdom that is acquired by study (philosophical and theological wisdom) and infused wisdom,

183

which is a gift of the Holy Ghost and linked with charity, the other declaring the perfection of charity to fall under the commandment, as the end to which every man ought to strive according to his degree.

As far as philosophy more particularly is concerned, the Encyclical unreservedly commends St. Thomas's (entirely Aristotelian) conception of the structure and essential divisions of the supreme form of knowledge in the natural order, and quotes this important passage from the *Commentary on the Ethics:*

" 'It is the function of the wise man to put things in order, because wisdom is primarily the perfection of reason and it is the characteristic of reason to know order; for although the sensitive faculties know some things absolutely, only the intellect or reason can know the relation one thing bears to another. The sciences therefore vary according to the various forms of order which reason perceives to be peculiar to each. The order which the consideration of reason establishes in its own peculiar activity pertains to rational philosophy or *logic,* whose function is to consider the order of the parts of speech in their mutual relations and in relation to the conclusions which may be drawn from them. It is for natural philosophy or *physics* to consider the order in natural things which human reason considers but does not itself institute, so that under natural philosophy we include also *metaphysics.*

But the order of voluntary acts is for the consideration of moral philosophy which is divided into three sections: the first considers the activities of the individual man in relation to their end and is called *monastics;* the second considers the activities of the family group or community and is called *economics;* the third considers the activities of the State and is called *politics*' (*In Ethic.,* lect. I).

"St. Thomas dealt thoroughly with all these several divisions of philosophy [the Pope proceeds], each according to its appropriate method, and, beginning with things nearest to us, rose step by step to things more remote, until he stood in the end 'on the topmost peak of all things . . . *in supremo rerum omnium vertice*' (*Contra Gent.,* ii, 56; iv, 1).

"His teaching with regard to the power or value of the human mind is irrefragable (*sanctum*). 'The human mind has a natural knowledge of being and the things which are in themselves part of being as such, and this knowledge is the foundation of our knowledge of first principles' (*Contra Gent.,* ii, 83). Such a doctrine goes to the root of the errors and opinions of those modern philosophers who maintain that it is not being itself which is perceived in the act of intellection, but some modification of the percipient: the logical consequence of such errors is agnosticism, which was so vigorously condemned in the Encyclical *Pascendi.*

"The arguments adduced by St. Thomas to prove the existence of God and that God alone is subsisting Being Itself are still to-day, as they were in the

185

Middle Ages, the most cogent of all arguments,[20] and clearly confirmed that dogma of the Church which was solemnly proclaimed at the Vatican Council and succinctly expressed by Pius X as follows: 'The certain knowledge of God as the first principle of creation and its last end and demonstrable proof of His existence can be inferred, like the knowledge of a cause from its effect, by the light of the natural reason, from creation, that is to say the visible works of creation' (Motu Proprio *Sacrorum Antistitum,* 1st September, 1910). The metaphysical philosophy of St. Thomas, although exposed to this day to the bitter onslaughts of prejudiced critics, yet still retains, like gold which no acid can dissolve, its full force and splendour unimpaired. Our Predecessor therefore rightly observed: 'To deviate from Aquinas, in metaphysics especially, is to run grave risk.' "

As for theology, the following remarkable passage should be borne in mind as showing how that science itself seeks to be completed and perfected in contemplation:

"For just as a man cannot really be said to know some distant country whose acquaintance is confirmed merely to a description of it, however accurate, but must have dwelt in it for some little time, so nobody can attain to an intimate knowl-

---

[20] An instructive comparison might be drawn between this grave papal declaration and the baseless assertions (due, if the truth be told, to a fundamental incomprehension of the mind of St. Thomas) made by modernist criticism, as certain Catholic philosophers conceive themselves able to restate it, against the arguments in question.

edge of God by mere scientific investigation, unless
he also dwells in the closest association with God."

And again on the theological work of St. Thomas:

"For in the first place he established apologetics
on a sound and genuine basis by defining exactly the
difference between the province of reason and
the province of faith and carefully distinguishing
the natural and the supernatural orders. When the
sacred Vatican Council, therefore, in determining
what natural knowledge of religion was possible,
affirmed the moral necessity of some divine revelation for sure and certain knowledge, and the absolute necessity of divine revelation for knowledge
of the mysteries, it employed arguments which
were borrowed precisely from St. Thomas. He insists that all who undertake to defend the Christian
faith shall hold sacrosanct the following principle
that: 'It is not mere folly to assent to the things
of faith, although they are beyond reason' (*Contra
Gent.*, i, 6). He shows that, although the articles
of belief are mysterious and obscure, the reasons
which persuade us to believe are nevertheless clear
and perspicuous, for, says he, 'a man would not
believe unless he saw that there were things to be
believed' (II–II, 1, 4), and he adds that, 'far from
being considered an impediment or a servile yoke
imposed upon men, faith should, on the contrary,
be reckoned a very great blessing, because faith
in us is a sort of beginning of eternal life' (*De
Verit.*, xiv, 2).

"The other part of theology, which is concerned

with the interpretation of dogmas, also found in St. Thomas by far the richest of all commentators: for nobody ever more profoundly penetrated or expounded with greater subtlety all the august mysteries, as, for example, the intimate life of God, the obscurity of eternal predestination, the supernatural government of the world, the faculty granted to rational creatures of attaining their end, the redemption of the human race achieved by Jesus Christ and continued by the Church and the sacraments, both of which the Angelic Doctor describes as 'relics, so to speak, of the divine Incarnation.'

"He also composed a substantial moral theology capable of directing all human acts in accordance with the supernatural last end of man. And as he is, as We have said, the perfect theologian, so he gives infallible rules and precepts of life not only for individuals, but for civil and domestic society as well, which is the object also of moral science, both economic and politic.[21]

"Hence those superb chapters in the second part of the *Summa Theologica* on paternal or domestic government, the lawful power of the State or the nation, natural and international law, peace and war, justice and property, laws and the obedience they command, the duty of helping individual citizens in their need and co-operating with all to secure the prosperity of the State both in the natural and the supernatural order. If these precepts

---

[21] This short passage, a concise statement of the subordination of politics to morals and the superior light of theology, showed by anticipation the remedy in the philosophy of St. Thomas for the *political naturalism* which has since been condemned by the Supreme Pontiff.

were religiously and inviolably observed in private life and public affairs and in the duties of mutual obligation between nations, nothing else would be required to secure mankind that 'peace of Christ in the kingdom of Christ' which the world so ardently longs for."

So the Encyclical *Studiorum Ducem* itself characterizes the function of the *wise architect* incumbent upon the Angelic Doctor in regard to the restoration of Christian culture in the modern world.

Finally,

"if we are to avoid the errors which are the source and fountain-head of all the miseries of our time, the teaching of Aquinas must be adhered to more religiously than ever. For St. Thomas refutes the theories propounded by Modernists in every sphere, in philosophy, by protecting, as We have reminded you, the force and power of the human mind and by demonstrating the existence of God by the most cogent arguments; in dogmatic theology, by distinguishing the supernatural from the natural order and explaining the reasons for belief and the dogmas themselves; in theology, by showing that the articles of faith are not based upon mere opinion but upon truth and therefore cannot possibly change; in exegesis, by transmitting the true conception of divine inspiration; in the science of morals, sociology and law, by laying down sound principles of legal and social, commutative and distributive, justice and explaining the relation between justice and charity; in the theory of asceticism by his precepts concerning the perfection of the Christian life and his confutation of the enemies of the religious orders in his own day. Lastly, against the much vaunted liberty of the human mind and its independence in regard to God he asserts the rights of primary Truth and the authority over us of the supreme Master. It is therefore clear why Modernists are so amply justified in fearing no Doctor of the Church so much as Thomas Aquinas.

"Accordingly, just as it was said to the Egyptians of old in time of famine: *Go to Joseph,* so that they should receive a supply of corn from him to nourish their bodies, so We now say to all such as are desirous of the truth: *Go to Thomas,* and ask him to give you from his ample store the food of substantial doctrine wherewith to nourish your souls unto eternal life."

Two things in the context seem to us particularly striking. In the first place the Church stakes everything, so to speak, on St. Thomas and his philosophy, and so proposes for our acceptance not any one particular truth but a whole *corpus* of doctrine. We should observe in the second place the dramatic accent in the entreaties she has continued ever since Leo XIII to address to her faithful on this head and still more to her clergy. She seems to consider the debate as one of immense importance, as a vital question for the interests of the Faith and civilization.

Why should this be so?

190

Because it is not with particular and defined heresies that we are confronted at the present day, but with a comprehensive universal heresy; it is the foundations which have given way and reason which is collapsing. There is no longer any belief in truth in the natural or the supernatural order, and human life is being divorced from truth; this is the core of the modernism which Pius X condemned in 1907 in the Encyclical *Pascendi* and described as "the cesspool of all errors." Such a danger must be encountered not with a particular truth but with the whole faith, so far as heaven is concerned, and all the light of the infused gifts, and, on earth, by a whole philosophy, by the whole of philosophy, comprehensively considered in its universality and doctrinal unity.

The various aspects of the essential harmony between dogma and reason are not to be studied in a few pages. Here I would merely recall the extreme solicitude with which the Church, who has yet far superior, far more beautiful objects to contemplate, is concerned to defend and guarantee the value and dignity of natural reason in which she admires a created participation of the God she loves, of the Light which enlighteneth every man coming into the world. In 1567 against Michel De Bay (*Baius*), in 1713 against Pasquier Quesnel, she asserted the validity of the knowledge of the moral law and the existence of God which the exercise of natural reason procured to the pagans. In 1840, she insisted that the Abbé Bautain, in 1855, that the Abbé Bonnetty, should acknowledge "that reasoning can prove with certainty the existence of God, the spirituality of the soul and the freedom of man," that "the use of the reason precedes faith and leads man to faith with the help of revelation and grace." In 1870, at the Vatican Council, she solemnly defined that:

"God, the first principle and ultimate End of all things, can be known with certainty (*certo cognosci*) by the natural light of human reason from created things" and, more precisely, that "His existence can be demonstrated (*adeoque demonstrari posse*) by means of the visible works of creation, as a cause by its effects." [22]

She, who has been the victim of so many calumnies by false reason, so safeguards reason against itself, when that erstwhile goddess in an access of philosophical frenzy has recourse to suicide to put an end to her sufferings.

All this is easily explained, if it is true that grace perfects nature and that man is naturally an animal endowed with reason. Destroy the force of reason and you destroy also the natural foundations them-

[22] Cf. the anti-Modernist oath prescribed by Pius X (Motu Proprio *Sacrorum Antistitum*, 1st September, 1910).

selves by which grace *takes* on the human being, you erect a divine building, exceedingly weighty, on ground already undermined. The Christian life is far from easy, and St. Christopher needs broad shoulders to bear the infant Jesus. It needs a sound mind to bear supernatural truth.

I do not say that it necessarily needs the mind of philosophers, a technically developed and cultivated mind. If Philosophy, with its choicest intellectual splendours, forms part of the treasure of the Church, is necessary to the integrity and full development of the doctrinal life on this earth, it is not necessary for every member of the faithful, at any rate for the simple and the unlettered. The truths of the Faith, on the other hand, are in themselves independent of every philosophical system (I say independent of every system, not indifferent in regard to every system), because descending directly from God they are superior to every philosophical conception. Christ nowhere philosophizes in the Gospel: He was wisdom incarnate and had no need to seek for it.

But what is necessarily required is the mind in its natural vigour, that spontaneous and naturally direct use of the mind which is called common sense.

Now it is the fundamental rectitude of common sense, the very health of the natural reason, which is affected and destroyed by the great errors which

193

have their origin in modern philosophy. The natural vigour of the mind and common sense, which the philosophers have destroyed, can, such being the case, be restored only if the mind rights itself philosophically, in the science of the superior truths naturally accessible to man. Faith and grace—*gratia sanans*—will help in this remedial work; they do not make it useless or superfluous, on the contrary they rather insist upon it.

What then are the most striking characteristics from our present point of view of the philosophy of St. Thomas?

That philosophy has already appeared to us as genuinely incorporated in the intellectual life of the Church, as the best suited to the Faith, as Pius X observed in his Motu Proprio *Doctoris Angelici,* as the instrument *par excellence* of theology. No other philosophical doctrine has, as a matter of fact, been able to take its place in the contexture of theology without causing some damage. Heretics themselves pay it this testimony. *"Tolle Thomam et dissipabo Ecclesiam"* exclaimed the Protestant Martin Bucer; and Jansenius: *"Fastidit Thomas, dum Augustinum degusto"* (as though it were a question of relishing what requires in the first place to be understood). Let it be observed in passing that this is a remarkable *indication* of the truth of Thomist philosophy: I said in the beginning of this chapter that theology,

THE COMMON DOCTOR

being a superior science, in itself independent of
every philosophy, must assume in its service of all
philosophical systems the system which in its hands
will be the best instrument of truth. Could it possibly be the best instrument of truth, if it were not
itself true?

But there is a second characteristic peculiar to the
philosophy of St. Thomas. It is *par excellence* the
philosophy of the mind, the philosophy of common
sense.[23]

Certainly not in the same sense as the philosophy
of the Scottish school. For it is not based upon the
authority of the common consent of mankind; it
reposes solely upon the evidence of the object.

In an altogether different sense; in this sense, that
common sense is itself an embryonic and rudimen-
tary philosophy, a philosophy which has not yet
reached a scientific state. Does common sense not
firmly believe that what is is, that the same thing
cannot be predicated at the same time as existent
and non-existent, that in affirmation or denial, if we
speak the truth, we are dealing with what is, that
whatever happens has a cause, that the sensible

---

[23] By *common sense* is here meant the intuition of first principles and
the first certitudes which, like a dowry bestowed by nature, attend on the
spontaneous exercise of reason. This common sense as natural *intellection*
must be carefully distinguished from the common sense of primitive
imagery, which conceives the earth as flat, the sun as revolving round the
earth, height and depth as absolute properties of space, etc., and has no
philosophical value whatsoever.

world exists, that man has a substantial self, that our wills are free, that the primordial laws of morality are universal, lastly, that the world did not make itself and that its Author is an intelligent being? Now this spontaneously direct reason, this common sense which precedes faith and without which the words which faith puts on our lips lose their significance for us, we rediscover in the philosophy of St. Thomas, but transfigured by the light of learning; it is the philosophy implicit in him; not only does the doctrine of St. Thomas demonstratively establish the conclusions instinctively laid down by common sense, but there is also a perfect continuity between its principles, even when they are most apparently disconnected and subtle, and the primary evidences of the intelligence in the wrapping of the certitudes of common sense.[24] Based upon objective evidence, subject to the most vigorous method, concerned to the point of scrupulosity for critical and analytical reflection, leading metaphysical reflection up the steepest and loftiest heights, Thomist philosophy is the discipline of wisdom which corresponds in the scientific order to the natural certitudes of reason. They perceive this clearly who, penetrating it after a long sojourn in the artificial paradises of modern philosophy, feel all the fibres of their mind

[24] Cf. R. Garrigou-Lagrange, *Le Sens Commun, la Philosophie de l'être et les formules Dogmatiques.* 3rd ed., Desclée De Brouwer, Paris.

tingle with a renewal of life. Here again we can observe in passing a remarkable indication of truth. For if the mind is worth anything at all—and if the mind is worth nothing, it were better to be a vegetable than a philosopher—is not the philosophy which develops best in the natural line of the mind also the most true?

The philosophy of St. Thomas is at the same time the only philosophy capable of maintaining and defending against every assault, the only philosophy which, in fact, undertakes to maintain and defend, the integrity of the mind, and to justify—and this is the specific function of metaphysical wisdom—the principles of human knowledge. The consequence is that we are compelled in the last resort by intellectual positions, which are much more definite now than they were a hundred or two hundred years ago owing to the development of modern philosophy, to make a choice between the two terms of this alternative: integral realism in the sense of St. Thomas or pure irrationality.

Thomism is the philosophy *par excellence* as far as faith and revealed truth are concerned, the philosophy *par excellence* as regards natural reason and common sense; it has many other characteristics, but those are the two which make it easiest for us to understand the unique confidence reposed in it by the Church.

Must it then be said that the Church has *canon-ized* the philosophy of St. Thomas? Yes, certainly, in the sense that she has included the teaching of that philosophy among the prescriptions of Canon Law. It must be said in that sense that the philosophy of St. Thomas is the philosophy of the Church, the philosophy employed by the Church in her own peculiar life, the philosophy she orders her masters to teach, the philosophy she would like to see adopted with an unceasingly manifested desire by her faithful.

But has she canonized it in the sense of imposing it upon the adhesion of minds in virtue of her doctrinal magistracy? No. From this point of view, no philosophy, that is to say no doctrine of purely human wisdom, could possibly be described, in strictness of terms, as "the Catholic philosophy." There can be no "philosophical system which a man must adopt in order to be a Christian." [25] The philosophy of St. Thomas is not a dogma, the Church can define as a truth *de fide* only what is contained, at least implicitly, in the divine deposit of revelation. Any particular truth professed by the Thomist philosophy may very well be so defined one day (if the Church considers that it was contained in the deposit of faith and cases have in fact already arisen) —but never the whole philosophy, the *corpus* of

[25] Cf A. D. Sertillanges, *Revue des Jeunes*, 25th August, 1921.

Thomist doctrine; and the truth in question will
never be defined as philosophical, because it can
only be defined as contained in the deposit of revelation. For by the very fact of the elevation of dogma
and its independence of every philosophical system,
any such truth will be raised above the vocabulary
and formulæ of philosophy, as, for instance, when
the Council of Vienne defined that the rational
soul is in itself and essentially the form of the human
body. Such a definition, as Pius IX explained in
1877, affirms only the substantial unity of human
nature, composed of two partial substances, the
body and the rational soul, it does not impose the
philosophical meaning, the strictly Aristotelian
meaning of the word *form*—although as a matter
of fact, but this is quite another thing which concerns our reason, we can find no other philosophical
doctrine except that of Aristotle which fully answers the fact.

However, as it was observed at the beginning of
this chapter, the doctrinal magistracy of the Church
is not strictly confined to definitions of faith, and
every Catholic should receive the philosophy of St.
Thomas for what it in fact is—a philosophy which
the Church has adopted for her own and which she
asserts to be "according to Christ" [26]—with the respect therefore due to such a pronouncement.

[26] Cf. p. 150, note.

But a philosophy is not imposed upon the mind by means of authority; to do so would be a defiance of the very nature of things, philosophy being essentially the work of reason.

The Church, acting as a perfect society with her own peculiar executive organs, orders her masters to teach the philosophy of St. Thomas, and by that very fact recommends the faithful to adhere to it; she throws every possible light upon that philosophy, makes use of every kind of signal, cries out: It is there you will find the running waters. She exercises no compulsion, forces nobody to go.

She is even exceedingly generous and forbearing towards her teachers, teachers being everywhere, as we know, a cross-grained, pernickety tribe.

Leo XIII in the Encyclical *Aeterni Patris* and Pius X in the Encyclical *Pascendi* had been at pains, as we have already seen,[27] to observe that:

"if there be any proposition too subtly investigated or too inconsiderately taught by the Doctors of the School, any tenet of theirs not strictly in conformity with subsequent discoveries or in any way improbable in itself, it is no part of Our intention to propose that for the imitation of Our age."

Certain teachers promptly took advantage of this exception to treat the very principles of St. Thomas,

[27] Cf. p. 145.

considered doubtless as sinning through excess of subtlety, as so much refuse.

Pius X, it will be remembered, protested energetically in the Motu Proprio *Doctoris Angelici* against such an abuse [28] and ordered teachers to be religiously faithful to the *principia et pronuntiata majora,* the principles and major theses, of the Thomist philosophy (an order later inscribed in the new code of Canon Law). Yet it might well be asked what those major theses are.

On the 27th July, 1914, the Congregation of Studies published by order of Pius X twenty-four theses which, it declared, "openly contain the principles and major theses of the philosophy of the holy Doctor." [29] It was the last public act of Pius X.

Certain teachers thereupon inquired if all the twenty-four theses were obligatory in their teaching. On the 7th March, 1916, the Congregation of Studies, which in the meantime had become the Congregation of Seminaries and Universities, while confirming that the twenty-four theses did in fact

[28] Cf. p. 146.
[29] [*Theses quaedam in doctrina S. Thomae Aquinatis contentae et a philosophiae magistris propositae, adprobantur. Acta Ap. Sedis,* vol. VI, p. 383. These twenty-four theses have been commented upon and explained by P. Guido Mattiussi, S.J. (†11th March, 1925) the draftsman, in the *Civiltà Cattolica* (1917) and translated into French by the Abbé Levillain under the title of *Les Points Fondamentaux de la Philosophie Thomiste,* Turin-Rome, 1926. Cf. also *Les vingt-quatre Thèses Thomistes* by Père Ed. Hugon, O.P., Paris, 1922. Tr.]

express the authentic doctrine of St. Thomas (*Omnes illae viginti quatuor theses philosophiae germanam S. Thomae doctrinam exprimunt*), replied by ordering them merely to be proposed in teaching as safe rules of guidance: "*proponantur veluti tutae normae directivae.*"

We should admire the caution (not unmixed with irony) with which the Church proceeds in the government of minds, because she knows the frailty of human nature. She imposes the teaching of the philosophy of St. Thomas on those to whom she entrusts the task of teaching; she declares that twenty-four theses, which she publishes, express the capital points of doctrine in the philosophy of St. Thomas; she is then asked if she imposes the teaching of these twenty-four theses, and her answer is "No—I do not impose them upon you." Because, she thinks, they will surely come to see that, if they must teach St. Thomas, they must also teach the twenty-four theses which faithfully express the mind of St. Thomas. "But so long as they do not see it. I will let them be. I will give them time to draw the consequences for themselves; and to convince themselves of the truth of what I ask them to teach on my behalf."

Does the Church impose on her faithful a sort of "ideological conformity" in philosophy? No.

THE COMMON DOCTOR

May a Catholic then consider the philosophy of St. Thomas as something which he is at liberty to contemplate with indifference, something proposing itself for his consideration exactly in the same way and in the same conditions as any other philosophical doctrine? No.

The philosophy of St. Thomas proposes itself, like every philosophical system, to the examination of our reason, but it is the only philosophy which proposes itself with the recommendation and the formidable co-efficient, so to speak, of being the philosophy which the mystical body of Christ, the Church of whom we are members, uses in her own peculiar intellectual life. If the authority of teachers plays in the generation of human knowledge the rôle mentioned in the early pages of this essay, if it has a rôle also, however secondary, in knowledge itself, how much more compelling should the authority of the Church be—and her example, perhaps, ever so much more than her behests, the very fact that in her own peculiar intellectual life she makes constant use of the philosophy of the common Doctor—to turn an attentive mind in his direction, to encourage it patiently to seek, under the bitter rind of scholasticism, the fruit of the promised knowledge. There is doubtless only one way of judging a philosophy for what it is worth and that is to study it in itself and to appraise its intrinsic evidence. But meanwhile, what an indication of it for a Christian to see the Church officially placing her trust in a man, in a Doctor! The reason is that in the case of St. Thomas, to quote the profound observation of John of St. Thomas,[30] something more important than St. Thomas is taken up and defended, *majus aliquid in sancto Thoma quam sanctus Thomas suscipitur et defenditur.* It is proper to remember that God in His most exalted works proceeds by way of privileges and exceptions and unique cases. He once sent His only begotten Son on earth, and gave Him a precursor. He once gave the Law through Moses—is there anything surprising in that He should once have given His Church a Doctor *par excellence* in philosophical and theological wisdom?

The indication referred to, while still remaining in regard to the actual philosophy of St. Thomas a merely extrinsic indication, something in the nature of a well-founded confidence rather than of absolute science, would yet acquire in the mind of anyone who conceived an adequate idea of the wisdom of the Church, the character of a certitude as

---

[30] [John of St. Thomas, Jean Poinsot, O.P., was born in Lisbon in 1589 and died at Fraga in Aragon in 1644. The Vivès edition of his *Cursus Philosophicus* (Paris, 10 vols., 1883–1886), is, unfortunately, textually very defective but a new edition has been prepared by Dom Reisci for Desclée a Cia, Rome. Cf. his *Isagoge ad theologiam D. Thomae*, which has been admirably adapted into French, with excellent notes, by M. Benoît Lavaud, O.P., under the title of *Introduction à la théologie de St. Thomas*, Blot. Paris, 1928. Tr.]

to the value of that philosophy considered as a whole, and beget an absolutely solid intellectual determination. Once again it is not a question of contriving a substitute for the labour of philosophical speculation, but of preparing and stimulating it; it is not a question of forcibly compelling adhesion to a philosophy, but of inviting inquirers, from love and compassion, to go and see the truth where the truth is to be found. That is the meaning of those great signals in the sky of which we have witnessed a succession since Leo XIII. *Come and see,* is always the way in which good tidings are announced. "We now say to all such as are desirous of the truth: *Go to Thomas.*" [31]

So the Catholic Church invites those who believe in her not to adapt texts selected here and there in the *Summa Theologica* to the benefit of any particular personal doctrine, but to go to St. Thomas in his living unity. She wants him to be the master of their philosophical education, the master to whom the pupil entrusts himself to learn how to think for himself and acquire knowledge. As she has appointed St. Thomas to the task of going and addressing the mind, so she urges the mind to go and listen to St. Thomas. It is to be wished that his modern disciples understood their duty in consequence. The time has long gone by for them to carp at Scotists and Oc-

[31] Pius XI. Encyclical *Studiorum Ducem.*

camists, Molinists, Augustinians, Suarezians and Vasquezians on scholastic questions which must now be considered as having been settled for centuries. (Such great questions are not to be despised, for to do so would be cowardice, and nobody is entitled to consider himself a philosopher who has not thoroughly investigated them, but other problems are more pressing.) The philosophy of St. Thomas seems to be entering a period of its development which is at once more apostolic and more laic; it is required by all the problems of culture. The mind, which needs it everywhere, would never forgive it for going to sleep at its post.

It insists upon a living Thomism, a system capable of taking part in the life of the world and working for the good of the world. In virtue of a profound law which can appear paradoxical only to a mind nourished on appearances, the more laic such a Thomism becomes, the more it sets to work in the profane sphere, the more will it simultaneously be of the Church. For if it is to proceed without altering its essence and with genuine efficacity to the extreme limits to which it is summoned, there must be transmitted through it a virtue which it derives from something more exalted than itself, from the energies of the Church of Christ. The presupposition is that a living, actual, active bond unites all that intellectual effort to the prayer of the contemplatives in their solitudes and charterhouses and that such work among men is really borne up by that prayer to God.

Those who follow St. Thomas in such a disposition will share in that sort of poverty of spirit which gave that greatest of Doctors the demeanour and simplicity of a child. They will not repose their confidence in their learning, they will put their trust in the God of compassion alone, to Whom they and their learning are remitted as instruments. They do not on that account stunt their learning, as happens whenever learning is used as an instrument to serve some human interest. They will on the contrary carefully preserve all its vigour and disinterestedness, for they will employ it only in the service of Him who conserves all things in their integrity and loyalty.

But because of this very poverty and such an instrumental rôle, they may hope effectively to serve the good of souls and the good of the human community: because they will order their effort to something above and beyond the human community, to the extension of the Kingdom of God and the evangelization of the world; an end which is more exalted than culture and on which culture itself depends.

As St. Thomas combated both Averroists and pseudo-Augustinians, so a double error must here be avoided: one error which may be situated under the sign of Cartesian optimism and which hopes for, nay, insists upon, a complete and perfect rational organization of the world, a stabilization of culture in a definitive natural perfection, as though human nature were not wounded and as though our end were not supernatural.

And another error which may be situated under the sign of Lutheran pessimism and which, despairing absolutely of the world and culture, abandons both to the powers of the Devil, as though we had not been really redeemed by Christ.

The Gospel tells us that we are in the world and not of the world; which is to say that the effort which we make in the world will remain incomplete in the world, but that we are nevertheless bound to make it all the more hopefully, in the assurance that it is completed elsewhere and that the little good we may be able to procure on this earth, and ever so much more our sufferings and our very infirmities are put to very good account by Him we love.

APPENDICES

APPENDIX I

CHRONOLOGICAL TABLES

The Life and Writings of St. Thomas

THE following tables are taken from a series of synopses drawn up by M. René Labergerie and shortly to be published in book form. To determine the catalogue of the authentic works and the chronological dates of their appearance (which are partly provisional, because scholars still disagree on many points and many important works are in course of publication), cf. more particularly Mandonnet's *Des écrits authentiques de St. Thomas,* Freiburg, 1910, 2nd ed.; the Introductions to the *Bibliographie thomiste,* Le Saulchoir, 1921; to the edition of the *Quaestiones disputatae,* Paris, 1925; the *Quaestiones quodlibetales,* Paris, 1926, and the *Opuscula omnia,* Paris, 1927; the *Chronologie des écrits scripturaires de Saint Thomas d'Aquin,* in the *Revue Thomiste* for Jan.–Feb., 1928, and following numbers; Grabmann's *Die echten Schriften des hl. Thomas von Aquin,* in Baeumker's *Beiträge,* vol. XXII, 1920; *Les Commentaires de Saint*

Thomas sur les ouvrages d'Aristote, in the *Annales de l'inst. sup. de phil. de Louvain,* vol. III, 1914; *die Aristoteles Kommentare des hl. Thomas von Aquin,* in *Mittelalterliches Geistesleben,* Munich, 1926; Bacic's *Introductio compendiosa in Opera S. Thomae Aquinatis,* Angelicum, 1925; Destrez, *Les disputes quodlibétiques de St. Thomas d'après la tradition manuscrite,* in *Mélanges thomistes,* Le Saulchoir, 1923; Synave's review of Destrez in *Bulletin thomiste,* May 1924; and the *Catalogue officiel des œuvres de Saint Thomas d'Aquin,* in *Archives d'hist. doctrinale et littéraire du moyen âge,* vol. III, 1928.

Scholars are still in disagreement as to the apocryphal nature of certain opuscula (not mentioned in the following tables) and the chronology of the works of St. Thomas and subsequent investigations will certainly modify some of the results there summarized; the chronology above all is provisional, and if the date of the scriptural writings seems to have been definitively fixed, very probably, by the work of Mandonnet, that of the commentaries upon Aristotle is still far from certain. For the chronology of these commentaries Mandonnet (Introduction to the *Bibliographie thomiste*) has been generally followed except so far as the commentaries upon the *Metaphysics,* the *Physics* and the *Ethics* are concerned. Mandonnet dates their composition to the period between 1265 and 1266; but the writing of such important works must have occupied several years of the first Italian period of teaching, perhaps from 1261 onwards, as Grabmann suggested in 1914. (Grabmann in 1926 attributes these commentaries to the second period of teaching in Paris, thus improbably overloading it.) Mandonnet attributes the commentary on the *de Anima* to 1266, but in this particular Grabmann has been followed. The latter suggests 1270–1272, a passage in this commentary seeming to refer clearly to the opusculum *De unitate intellectus*.

N.B.—1. The bracket on the right of a title indicates that the date of composition has not been definitively ascertained and must be attributed to the period included within the bracket.

2. The arrow on the left of a title indicates that the time taken in composition extends throughout the period included.

3. A date in parenthesis indicates that the period of composition extends beyond the limits of the table and down to the date in question.

1225–1252

PLACES AND DATES	PHILOSOPHY	PHILOSOPHI- CAL AND THEOLOGICAL SCHOOL	THEOLOGY	SCRIPTURE	VARIOUS
a. Italy					
1225–45					
1225					
Roccasecca					birth
1230					
Monte Cassino					oblate
1239					
Roccasecca					student in arts
Naples					
1244					
Naples					Dominican habit
Aquapendente					arrest
Roccasecca	de PROPOSIT. ⎤ MODALIBUS de FALLACIIS ⎥				internment
1245	⎦				set free
					departure for Paris
β. France					
Germany					
1245–52					
1245					
Paris					Convent; pupil of Al- bert the Great
1248					
Cologne			de DIVINIS ⎤ NOMINIBUS ⎥		
1252			⎦		departure from Cologne

1252-1259

PLACES AND DATES	PHILOSOPHY	PHILOSOPHICAL AND THEOLOGICAL SCHOOL	THEOLOGY	SCRIPTURE	VARIOUS
Paris					
1252	de ENTE et ESSENTIA		Liber MANDA-TORUM DEI		bachelor in biblical studies
1254			in IV lib. SEN-TENTIARUM		COLLATIO-NES DOMINICALES FESTIVAE QUADRAGES.
1255	de PRINCIPIIS NATURAE				
1256		QUODLIBET VII Quaest. disp. de OPERE MANUALI de SENS. SACR. SCRIPT. de VERITATE	RIGANS MONTES	in ISAIAM	licentiate in theology
1257	de HEBDOMA-DIBUS BOETII	QUODLIBET VIII	Contra IMPUGNANT. DEI CULTUM de TRINITATE BOETII	in MAT-THÆUM	
1258		QUODLIBET IX — X			
1259		QUODLIBET XI	SUMMA c. GENTES		(1264)
JUNE			(1260)		departure for Italy

215

PLACES AND DATES	PHILOSOPHY	PHILOSOPHI- CAL AND THEOLOGICAL SCHOOL	THEOLOGY	SCRIPTURE	VARIOUS
Anagni					
1259		Quaest. disp. de POTENTIA		in CANTIC. CANTICOR.	COLLATIO- NES in Iam IIam
1260				in EPISTOLAS PAULI (1)	DECRET.
1261			de RATIONI- BUS FIDEI		
Orvieto	in VIII lib. PHYSIC.		de ART. FIDEI et SACRA- MENT.		
	in XII lib. METAPHYS.				
	in X lib. ETHIC.				
1262			de EMPTIONE et VENDI- TIONE	CATENA (in Matth.)	Offic. CORP. CHRISTI Sermo de —.
1263		Quaest. disp. de MALO	Contra ERRORES GRAECORUM		
1264				CATENA (in Marc.) (in Joh.) (in Luc.)	
1265		DECLARATIO CVIII QUAEST.	in I SENTENT. (II) de REGIMINE PRINC.		
Rome	in lib. de SENSU ET SENSATO				
1266		Quaest. disp. de NATURA BEATITUDINIS	SUMMA THEO- LOGICA Ia Pars		
1267	in lib. de MEMORIA ET REMIN.				
Viterbo				in THRENOS in JEREMIAM	
1268	in POST. ANALYTIC.	Quaest. disp. de UNIONE VERBI			SERMONES (1273)
	in IV lib. POLITICOR.				
NOVEMBER					departure for Paris

IV.—SECOND PERIOD OF TEACHING IN PARIS

1269-1272

PLACES AND DATES	PHILOSOPHY	PHILOSOPHI- CAL AND THEOLOGICAL SCHOOL	THEOLOGY	SCRIPTURE	VARIOUS
Paris					
1269	le REGIMINE JUDÆOR.	de SECRETO	de PERFEC- TIONE VITAE SPIR.	in JOB	SERMONES
	de OCCULT. OP. NAT.	QUODLIBET I	SUMMA THEOLOGICA Ia-IIae		
	in lib. de CAUSIS	— II	de JUDICIIS ASTROR		
	in IV lib. METEOR.	Quaest. disp. de SPIRIT. CREAT.	de SORTIBUS		
	in PERIHER- MENEIAM	de ANIMA	de FORMA ABSOL.		
1270	de UNITATE INTEL.	QUODLIBET III	Contra RE- TRAHENTES a RELIGIONIS INGR.	in JOHANNEM	
	in III lib. de ANIMA	— XII			
	de ÆTER- NIT. MUNDI	Quaest. disp. de VIRTUTI- BUS			
1271		ARTICULI ITER. REM.	SUMMA THEOLO- GICA IIa-IIae		
		DECLARA- TIONES			
		XLII QUAEST.			
		XXXV —			
		VI —			
		QUODLIBET IV			
		— V			
		Quaest. disp. de PUERIS in RELIGIONE ADM.			
1272		QUODLIBET VI			(1273)
APRIL					departure for Italy

217

PLACES AND DATES	PHILOSOPHY	PHILOSOPHI-CAL AND THEOLOGICAL SCHOOL	THEOLOGY	SCRIPTURE	VARIOUS
Florence 1272					SERMONES
Naples	in lib. de CAELO et MUNDO		SUMMA THEO-LOGICA IIIa Pars	in PSALMOS in EPISTOLAS PAULI (II)	
	in lib. de GENERAT. et CORRUPT.		COMPEN-DIUM THEO-LOGIAE		
	de SUBSTAN-TIIS SEPA-RATIS				
1273	de MIXTIO-NE ELE-MENTOR.				COLLATIO-NES: de PATER-NOST.
					de AVE MARIA
	de MOTU CORDIS				de CREDO de X PRAE-CEP.
1274 *Monte Cassino*		RESPONS. ad BERNARD. ABB.	Works of UNCERTAIN DATE or DISPUTED AUTHENTICITY:— (i) EPIST. de MODO STUDENDI (ii) PIAE PRECES (ii) de DIVINIS MORIBUS		
Fossanova 7th MARCH					† death

APPENDIX II

TESTIMONIES OF THE SUPREME PONTIFFS[1]

Alexander IV (1254–1261)	9–23	7–24
Urban IV (1261–1264)	24–30	24–28
Clement IV (1265–1268)	31–36	29–31
Gregory X (1271–1276)	37–41	32–33
Innocent V (1276)	42–44	34–35
Nicholas III (1277–1280)	47–50	36–38
Martin IV (1281–1285)	51 P	38–39
Honorius IV (1285–1287)	52–53	39–40
Nicholas IV (1288–1292)	54 P	40–41
Celestine V (1294)	55 P	41
Boniface VIII (1294–1303)	56–57	42–43
Benedict XI (1303–1304)	58–59 P	43
Clement V (1305–1314)	60	44
John XXII (1316–1344)	61–69	44–53
1st March, 1318. Declares his doctrine miraculous. "He alone enlightened the Church more than all other doctors." 18th July, 1323. Bull of Canonization: "Redemptionem misit Dominus."	62	45
Benedict XII (1335–1342)	70 P	53–54
Clement VI (1342–1352)	71–78	54–61
1346. Orders the Friars Preachers not to deviate from the doctrine of St. Thomas.		
Innocent VI (1355–1362)	79	62

[1] Cf. *Sanctus Thomas Aquinas, "Doctor Communis" Ecclesiae*, by Sir J. J. Berthier, O.P., vol. I: *Testimonia Ecclesiae; Romae*, 1914. The column on the left refers to the paragraphs, that on the right to the pages, of the volume. The letter P indicates an explicit testimony to the Order of Preachers, referring implicitly to St. Thomas.

Urban V (1362–1370)	80–86	62–66
Gregory XI (1370–1378)	87–88	66–67
Urban VI (1378–1389)	89 P	68
Boniface IX (1389–1404)	90	68–69
Innocent VII (1404–1406)	91	70
6th July, 1406. Confirms the doctrine of the Friars Preachers which is the doctrine of St. Thomas; Const. "Decens reputamus."	91	70
Gregory XII (1406–1415)	92	71
Alexander V (1409–1410)	93	71–72
John XXIII (1410–1415)	94	72
Martin V (1417–1431)	95 P	73–74
Eugenius IV (1431–1447)	96–97	74–76
Nicholas V (1447–1455)	98–99	76–78
Calixtus III (1455–1458)	100–101	78–80
Pius II (1458–1464)	102	80–81
Paul II (1464–1471)	103 P	81–82
Sixtus IV (1471–1484)	104	82–83
Innocent VIII (1484–1492)	105	83–84
Alexander VI (1492–1503)	106	84
Julius II (1503–1513)	108 P	85–86
Leo X (1513–1521)	109–111 P	86–87
Clement VII (1523–1534)	113–115 P	88–90
Paul III (1534–1549)	116–118 P	90–92
Julius III (1550–1555)	119 P	93
Paul IV (1555–1559)	121	94–95
Pius IV (1559–1565)	122	95–96
Pius V (1566–1572)	123–125	97–101
11th April, 1567. Proclaims St. Thomas Doctor in the Const. "Mirabilis Deus."	124	97
1570. Orders an edition of the complete works of St. Thomas.	125	100
Gregory XIII (1572–1585)	126–127 P	101–103
Sixtus V (1585–1590)	128–130	103–106
Clement VIII (1592–1605)	134–140	108–115
1594. Recommends the Fathers		

APPENDICES

4th August, 1880. Appoints St. Thomas universal patron of Catholic schools. Brief: "Cum hoc sit."   238–242   208–211

30th December, 1892. Invites members of the Society of Jesus to follow the teaching of St. Thomas. Brief: "Gravissime Nos."   318–325   244–252

25th November, 1898. The same invitation is addressed to the Friars Minor.   352   264

9th May, 1895. Approves the new statutes of the Roman Academy of St. Thomas. Apostolic letter: "Constitutiones."   341   258–260

Pius X (1903–1914)   366–388   271–280
    680–682   695–702

8th September, 1907. Encyclical: "Pascendi."   376   276

1st September, 1910. Motu Proprio: "Doctoris Angelici."   680–681   695–699

27th July, 1914. Publication of the XXIV Thomist theses.   682   699–702

Benedict XV (1914–1922)

31st December, 1914. Motu Proprio: "Non Multo" on the Roman Academy of St. Thomas.

7th March, 1916. Answer given by the Congregation of Seminaries and Universities on the XXIV theses.

27th May, 1917. Promulgation of the new Code of Canon Law. (Can. 1366 § 2: "Teachers shall adhere religiously to the method, doctrine and principles" of St. Thomas.)

29th June, 1921. Encyclical: "Fausto appetente die."

APPENDICES

Pius XI

1st August, 1922. Apostolic letter on the education of the clergy.

29th June, 1923. Encyclical "Studiorum Ducem" for the sixth centenary of St. Thomas.

APPENDIX III

THREE PAPAL DOCUMENTS

Encyclical *Aeterni Patris*
Motu Proprio *Doctoris Angelici*
Encyclical *Studiorum Ducem*

I

AETERNI PATRIS

ENCYCLICAL LETTER OF OUR MOST HOLY
LORD POPE LEO XIII ON THE SCHOLASTIC
PHILOSOPHY

*To All Our Venerable Brethren,
the Patriarchs, Primates, Archbishops and Bishops
of the Catholic World
in grace and communion with the Apostolic See,
Leo XIII, Pope,
Venerable Brethren,
Greeting and the Apostolic Benediction.*

THE Only Begotten Son of the Eternal Father, Who
appeared on earth to bring salvation and the light of
divine wisdom to the human race, conferred a truly

great and wonderful benefit upon the world when, as He was about to ascend again into Heaven, He bade His Apostles "go and teach all nations" [1] and left the Church which He had founded to be the common and supreme teacher of all peoples. For men, whom the truth had made free, were to be preserved by the truth: and the fruits of the heavenly doctrines, through which man obtained salvation, would not have lasted long, if Christ Our Lord had not appointed a perpetual authority to teach men's minds the faith. The Church, indeed, established upon the promises and imitating the charity of her divine Founder, has carried out His orders in such a way that her consistent object and most earnest desire have ever been to teach religion and unceasingly to battle with error. The unwearying labours of the entire episcopate have been directed to that end, no less than the laws and decrees enacted by the Councils and, above all, the daily solicitude of the Roman Pontiffs, whose right and duty it is, as the successors in the primacy of St. Peter, the Prince of the Apostles, to teach and confirm their brethren in the faith.

Inasmuch, however, as the minds of the faithful of Christ are wont to be cheated, the Apostle warns us, "by philosophy and vain deceit," [2] and the purity

---

[1] *Matt.*, xxviii, 19.
[2] *Coloss.*, ii, 8.

of the faith so to be corrupted among men, the supreme pastors of the Church have ever considered it their duty to promote true science with all their strength and at the same time to be particularly vigilant to see that all forms of human knowledge, but philosophy especially, on which the proper understanding of the other sciences largely depends, be taught in accordance with the Catholic Faith. We briefly drew your attention, Venerable Brethren, to this amongst other things, in the first Encyclical Letter We had occasion to address to you; but the importance of the subject and the condition of the times compel Us to address you once more on the method of teaching philosophical studies in such a way as shall most fitly correspond with the blessing of faith and be consonant with the respect due to the human sciences themselves.

Anyone considering the critical state of the times in which we live and reflecting upon the condition of public and domestic affairs will easily perceive that a fruitful cause of the evils which actually oppress us and others which we may reasonably apprehend is to be found in the fact that erroneous theories respecting our duty to God and our responsibilities as men originally propounded in philosophical schools, have gradually permeated all ranks of society and secured acceptance among the majority of men. For as it is ingrained by nature in man to be guided by reason in conduct, the will is apt to follow quickly any error which the mind may make; so erroneous theories whose seat is in the mind come to influence human actions and pervert them. If, on the contrary, the minds of men are sound and securely based on solid, true principles, innumerable benefits accrue to the public and private advantage.

We do not certainly attribute such power and authority to human philosophy as to consider it capable of dispelling or eradicating every error whatsoever: for just as, when the Christian religion was first instituted, the world was restored to its primeval dignity by the diffusion of the admirable light of faith, "not in the persuasive words of human wisdom, but in shewing of the spirit and power," [3] so also now we must expect the minds of men, once the darkness or error has been dissipated, to be restored to sanity more particularly by the all-powerful virtue and assistance of God. Such natural help, however, as the benevolence of the divine wisdom, which ordereth all things mightily and sweetly, offers mankind is not to be despised or neglected, and of such help the sound use of philosophy is undoubtedly the most important kind.

[3] *I Cor.*, ii, 4.

For God has not endowed the human mind with reason to no purpose; and the added light of faith, so far from extinguishing or diminishing the vigour of the mind, rather on the contrary perfects it and by increasing its strength makes it the more capable of comprehending higher things.

The very nature of divine Providence therefore requires that the assistance of human science also be enlisted for the purpose of recalling nations to the faith and salvation, and the monuments of antiquity testify that such a proceeding is both commendable and prudent and was the habitual practice of the Fathers of the Church. They were wont to attribute no small or slender part to reason and the great Augustine briefly sums it up "in attributing to this science the power of begetting, nourishing, defending and consolidating . . . most salutary faith." [4]

For, in the first place, philosophy, if rightly practised as it is practised by the wise, is a means of preparing and smoothing the way, as it were, to the true faith and suitably disposing the minds of its disciples for the reception of revelation; for this reason it was not undeservedly described by the Ancients at one time as a "preparatory education for the Christian faith," [5] at another as "a prelude to

[4] *De Trinit.*, XIII, i.
[5] Clem. Alexandr., *Strom.* I, xvi; VIII, iii.

228

and auxiliary of Christianity,[6] at another again as "the guide to the Gospel." [7]

And truly, so far as divine things are concerned, God in His infinite goodness has not only made clear to us by the light of faith truths which the human mind unaided is incapable of grasping, but has also manifested to us other truths not wholly inaccessible to reason in such a way that, sanctioned by His authority, they should be immediately perceptible by all men without any admixture of error. Hence it is that certain truths, either divinely proposed for our belief or closely connected with the doctrines of the faith, have been acknowledged by the mere natural light of reason, demonstrated with appropriate proofs and vindicated even by pagan philosophers. "For the invincible things of him," in the words of the Apostle, "from the creation of the world, are clearly seen, being understood by the things that are made: his eternal power also and divinity: [8] and the gentiles who have not the law . . . nevertheless shew the work of the law written in their hearts. . . ." [9] It is eminently fitting to convert these truths which the wisdom even of the pagan philosophers has discovered to the use and benefit of revealed doctrine so as to show that in

---

[6] Orig., *Ad Gregor, Thaum.*
[7] Clem. Alexandr., *Strom.* I., v, *"Ad Evangelium paedagogus."*
[8] *Rom.*, i, 20.
[9] *Ibid.*, ii, 14–15.

fact human wisdom and the very testimony of its opponents bear witness to the Christian faith.

Such a method of procedure is certainly not of recent introduction but of ancient use and it was the common practice of the holy Fathers of the Church. Nay more, those venerable witnesses to, and guardians of, religious traditions discerned a type and prefiguration of it, as it were, in the fact that the Hebrews, on their departure from Egypt, were ordered to take with them the silver and gold vessels and precious vestments of the Egyptians, that such furniture, which had formerly been employed in the service of ignoble rites and superstition, should suddenly change use and be dedicated to the worship of the true God. Gregory of neo-Caesarea praises Origen [10] for ingeniously selecting a number of ideas from the pagan philosophers and converting them with consummate dexterity, like so many weapons wrested from the enemy, to the defence of Christian wisdom and the destruction of superstition. Both Gregory of Nazianzen [11] and Gregory of Nyssa [12] commend and approve a like method of argument as practised by Basil the Great. Jerome applauds it in the case of Quadratus, a disciple of the Apostles, of Aristides and Justin and

[10] *Orat. Paneg. ad Orig.*
[11] Vit. Moys.
[12] *Carm.* I. *Iamb.* 3.

Irenaeus and countless others.[13] Augustine no less: "Surely we can see," exclaims the great Doctor, "what a heavy load of gold and silver and precious vestments Cyprian, that gentlest of doctors and most blessed of martyrs, bore with him out of Egypt? Lactantius also, and Victorinus, Optatus and Hilary? And not to mention the living, the innumerable Greeks?" [14] Now if natural reason could produce such a rich harvest of doctrine before being fertilized by the virtue of Christ, it will surely produce one still more fruitful now that the grace of the Saviour has restored and increased the natural faculties of the human mind. Is it not plain to all men what a smooth and easy way is opened to the faith by such a method of philosophizing?

The utility to be derived from this kind of philosophy is not, however, circumscribed within such narrow limits. And the words of divine wisdom in Holy Writ gravely rebuke the folly of men "who, by these good things that are seen, could not understand him that is, neither by attending to the works have acknowledged who was the workman." [15] We are therefore indebted to human reason in the first place for this great, pre-eminent benefit, that it enables us to demonstrate the existence of God: "for

[13] *Epist. ad Magn.*
[14] *De Doctr. Christ.*, II, xl.
[15] *Wisdom.*, xiii, 1.

231

by the greatness of the beauty, and of the creature,
the Creator of them may be seen so as to be known
thereby." [16] In the second place, it shows that God
is singularly excellent in the sum of all perfections,
in His infinite wisdom to begin with, which nothing
can escape, and in His supreme justice, against which
no corrupt affection can ever prevail, and that God,
therefore, is not only truthful but Truth itself, as
incapable of deceiving as of being deceived. The
clear consequence is that human reason is disposed
to place the most ample confidence and authority
in the word of God. Reason similarly declares that
the doctrine of the Gospel was manifested from the
very beginning by certain marvellous signs, so many
infallible indications, as it were, of infallible truth;
and that those, therefore, who believe in the Gospel,
so far from doing so rashly like men following "cun-
ningly devised fables," [17] have submitted their minds
and judgments in absolutely rational obedience to
the divine authority. Reason also clearly shows—
and this is no less important—that the Church established by Christ, "by reason of her marvellous
expansion, eminent sanctity and inexhaustible fecundity in all places, her Catholic unity and unbroken stability, is," as the Vatican Council
declared, "a great and perpetual motive of be-

16 *Ibid.*, xiii, 5.
17 *II Peter*, i, 16.

lief, an irrefragable testimony to her divine mission." [18]

Once the foundations have been thus well and
truly laid, the practice of philosophy can still render
permanent service of many kinds, more particularly
by investing and endowing sacred theology with the
nature, habit and character of genuine science. For
it is of absolutely capital importance in the case of
this most noble branch of learning that the many
different parts which compose the heavenly teaching be gathered into one body, as it were; so that,
conveniently arranged each in its own place and derived each from its own peculiar principles, they
may be joined together in an appropriate connexion
and all and singular confirmed by the same un-
answerable arguments.—Nor is that more exact and
fruitful knowledge of the articles of belief, that
more intelligent appreciation, so far as possible, of
the very mysteries of faith, which Augustine and
the rest of the Fathers both commended and strove
to acquire and which the Vatican Council itself has
declared to be most beneficial,[19] to be passed over
in silence or lightly regarded. Such knowledge and
appreciation are certainly more easily and more
abundantly acquired by those who combine integrity of morals and zeal for the faith with a mind
well disciplined in philosophy, especially as that

[18] *Const. dogm. de Fide cath.*, 3.

233

same Vatican Council also teaches that such an understanding of sacred dogmas ought to be sought "both in the analogy with things which are objects of natural knowledge and in the mutual relation between the mysteries themselves and the ultimate end of man." [19]

Lastly, it is the function of the philosophical sciences religiously to protect the truths of divine revelation and to resist the attacks of those who dare to assail them. It is therefore the great glory of philosophy that it should be considered the bulwark of faith and the strong rampart of religion. "The doctrine of the Saviour is, indeed," as Clement of Alexandria declares, "perfect in itself and lacking nothing, because it is the virtue and the science of God. The support of Greek philosophy adds nothing to the force and power of truth; but inasmuch as it invalidates the arguments adduced by sophists against truth and scatters the cunning snares they lay to catch it, that philosophy has been described as the fence and prop of the vine." [20] Indeed, just as the enemies of the Catholic name in their warfare against religion borrow their weapons for the most part from philosophy, so the champions of the divine sciences also betake themselves to the arsenal of philosophy for many means of defending the

[19] *Constit. cit.*, 4.
[20] *Strom.* I, xx.

dogmas of revelation. And it is not to be accounted a meagre triumph for the Christian faith that human reason itself should be able to repel with power and ease the weapons which its adversaries have massed with all the cunning of human reason to do it injury. St. Jerome recalls in writing to Magnus [21] that this was the form of tactics in religious warfare adopted by the Apostle of the Gentiles himself: "The leader of the Christian army, the invincible orator, Paul, in pleading the cause of Christ, skilfully turned a chance inscription into an argument for the faith: for he had learned from the true David to wrest the enemy's sword out of his hand and with his own weapon to cut off the proud Goliath's head."

And the Church herself not only counsels Christian doctors to seek such assistance from philosophy but even orders them instantly to do so.

The Fifth Lateran Council [1512–1517] after declaring "that every statement contrary to the truth of revealed faith is absolutely false, because one truth cannot contradict another truth," [22] orders teachers of philosophy to practise assiduously the art of refuting specious arguments; because, as Augustine says, "if any argument, however subtle, be alleged against the authority of Holy Writ, it

[21] *Epist. ad Magn.*
[22] In the Bull *Apostolici regiminis.*

235

can deceive only by its appearance of truth, for absolutely true it cannot be." [23]

But, if philosophy is to bring forth such precious fruit as We have mentioned, it is absolutely essential that it never deflect from the path followed by the venerable Fathers of antiquity and sanctioned by the solemn authority of the Vatican Council. That is to say that, inasmuch as it is clear that we have to accept many truths of the supernatural order far beyond the comprehension of even the acutest mind, the human reason, conscious of its own frailty, must be careful not to venture out of its depths or to deny those truths or judge them by its own standards or interpret them according to its own caprice; it must rather receive them with a full and humble faith, and consider it the highest honour to be admitted in the capacity of a humble attendant or waiting-maid into familiarity with the heavenly doctrines, and by the gracious kindness of God howsoever to approach them. As regards those heads of doctrine, however, which the human mind can naturally perceive, it is only right that philosophy should use its own method, its own principles and arguments, but yet in such a way as not to seem boldly to reject the divine authority. As it is clear that the things which are made known to us by revelation are certainly true and that things con-

[23] Epist. cxliii *ad Marcellin*, 7.

trary to faith are equally repugnant to right reason, the Catholic philosopher must know that he will be doing violence to the rights of faith and reason alike, if he adopts any conclusion he knows to be repugnant to revealed doctrine.

We are well aware that there are many persons who, unduly exalting the faculties of human nature, contend that, if the human mind once submits to divine authority, it falls from its native dignity and, bowed beneath the yoke of a kind of slavery, is greatly retarded and impeded in its progress to the summit of truth and excellence. Such contentions are replete with error and illusion; and their sole object is to induce men, with the utmost stupidity and not without rendering themselves liable to the charge of ingratitude, to repudiate more exalted truths and wilfully to reject the divine blessing of faith, the source of all good even to civil society. The fact is that the human mind, being circumscribed within defined and very narrow limits, is therefore liable to innumerable errors and ignorance of many things. The Christian faith, on the other hand, being based upon the authority of God, is the most certain teacher of truth and anyone following it is not enmeshed in the snares of error or tossed about on the waves of fluctuating opinions. Those therefore are the best philosophers who combine the pursuit of philosophy with dutiful obedience to the

Christian faith, for the splendour of the divine truths irradiating the soul is a help also to the intelligence; it not only does not deprive it of the least degree of its dignity, but even brings it an increase of nobility, acuteness and strength.

They therefore exercise their reason worthily and most usefully who sharpen the edge of their minds in refuting theories repugnant to the faith and proving such as are congruent with the faith; in the former case they discover the cause of the error and discern the flaw in the arguments upon which such theories are based: in the latter, they acquire powerful arguments by which they may be convincingly demonstrated and proved to the satisfaction of every thinking man. Anyone denying that the riches of the mind are increased and its faculties developed by such practice and exercise must necessarily uphold the foolish contention that the distinction between good and bad is profitless for the progress of the mind. The Vatican Council therefore rightly asserts the exceptional benefits which the faith procures for reason in these terms: "Faith frees reason from errors, protects and enriches it with many kinds of knowledge." [24] A man, therefore, instead of inveighing against faith as the enemy of reason and natural truths, would, if he were wise, give

[24] *Constit. Dogm. de Fide Cath.*, 4.

worthy thanks to God and greatly rejoice that, amid so many causes of ignorance and so many shoals of error, the light of the most holy faith shone upon him, like a friendly star, beckoning him beyond all peril of going astray into the haven of truth.

Now if you consider, Venerable Brethren, the history of philosophy, you will find confirmation of everything which We have just said. Even those who were accounted the wisest of the ancient philosophers, lacking the blessing of faith, committed many grievous errors. For you are aware how many false and absurd propositions, how many uncertain and dubious theories they advanced (with some few true) concerning the real nature of divinity, the origin of creation, the government of the world, the divine knowledge of the future, the principle and cause of evil, the last end of men and eternal happiness, the virtues and the vices and other doctrines, true and certain knowledge of which is of the most absolute necessity to man.

The early Fathers and Doctors of the Church, on the other hand, who realized that it was part of the divine plan that human knowledge also should be renewed by "Christ the power of God and the wisdom of God," [25] "in whom are hid all the treasures

[25] I *Cor.*, i, 24.

of wisdom and knowledge," [26] undertook to investigate the works of the ancient philosophers and to compare their teaching with the doctrines of revelation. They adopted with sound discernment every truthful statement and wise opinion they could find, connecting or rejecting the rest. For just as God in His good providence raised up valiant martyrs for the defence of the Church, prodigies of magnanimity against the cruelty of oppressors, so He opposed men pre-eminent in wisdom against false philosophers or heretics to defend the treasure of divine revelation with the help of human reason itself. In the earliest days of the Church, Catholic doctrine encountered many determined adversaries who, deriding the dogmas and institutions of Christians, affirmed that the gods were many, that the material world was without principle or cause, and that the course of events was determined by some blind force and fatal necessity, not governed by any design of divine Providence. Men of wisdom, APOLOGISTS as they are called, speedily engaged the professors of such senseless philosophy and, with faith to guide them, drew arguments even from human wisdom to prove that only one God, excellent in all manner of perfection, was to be worshipped, that all things had been created out of nothing by His omnipotent power, subsist by His wisdom, and are

[26] *Coloss.*, ii, 3.

impelled and directed each to its appropriate end.

ST. JUSTIN MARTYR claims first place among them. He attended by way of experiment the most renowned academies of Greece and after having convinced himself that a full draught of truth was not to be drained, as he himself said, from any other source than revealed doctrine, he embraced it with all the ardour of his soul, cleared it of calumnies, vehemently and voluminously defended it before the Roman Emperors and reconciled with it many propositions of Greek philosophy. QUADRATUS and ARISTIDES, HERMIAS and ATHENAGORAS lent their valiant help almost about the same time. IRENAEUS, the indomitable martyr and Pontiff of the Church in Lyons, gained no less renown for the same reason by strenuously refuting perverse theories from the East, disseminated broadcast throughout the Roman Empire by the activity of the Gnostics, "explaining"—it is St. Jerome who tells us—"the origin of every single heresy and from what philosophical source it was derived."[27] The controversies of CLEMENT OF ALEXANDRIA are familiar to everyone and honourably referred to by St. Jerome in the following words: "Do they show the slightest trace of ignorance? Do they not contain the very essence of philosophy?" Clement was a most voluminous writer upon an incredible variety of subjects and his

[27] *Epist. ad Magn.*

241

works are most useful for the composition of a history of philosophy, the proper exercise of the art of dialectic, and the reconciliation of reason and faith. He was succeeded by ORIGEN, an illustrious teacher in the school of Alexandria and profoundly learned in the theories of Greek and Oriental philosophers, the author of innumerable works of consummate erudition admirably suited to the explanation of Holy Writ and the exposition of sacred dogmas. Although not entirely free from error, at any rate as they have come down to us, they nevertheless contain a great body of opinions by which natural truths are increased in number and strength.

TERTULLIAN controverted heretics with the authority of Holy Scripture and, changing his weapons, fought philosophers with philosophy. He refuted the philosophers with such acumen and erudition that he could openly and confidently taunt them with not being a match for him, whatever they might think, in learning or in knowledge.[28] ARNOBIUS also in the books he published *adversus Gentes* and LACTANTIUS more particularly in his *Institutiones Divinae*, strenuously endeavoured with equal eloquence and vigour to persuade men to accept the dogmas and precepts of Catholic wisdom, not so much by destroying philosophy as was the

---

[28] *"Neque de scientia, neque de disciplina, ut putatis, aequamur."* Apol., § 46.

way of the Academicians, as by appropriating to overthrow their opponents arguments drawn from their own mutual disputes.[29]

The great ATHANASIUS, and CHRYSOSTOM, prince of orators, have left us writings on the human soul and the divine attributes and other questions of the utmost importance, so excellent in the universal judgement that nothing apparently could possibly be added to their abundance and subtlety. And to avoid the prolixity of enumerating each and everyone, We will add to the number of most eminent men already mentioned merely BASIL THE GREAT and the two GREGORIES. They came from Athens, then the home of human culture. They were learned in the whole range of philosophy, and they devoted the wealth of doctrine which each had acquired by passionate study to the refutation of heretics and the instruction of Christians.

AUGUSTINE, however, would seem to have wrested the palm from all. Pre-eminent in intellect and thoroughly imbued with sacred and profane learning alike, he did battle resolutely against all the errors of his age, and his superb faith was equalled only by his learning. What aspect of philosophy did he leave untouched? Or rather, what aspect did he not most diligently investigate? At one time he would discover to the faithful the most recondite

[29] De Op. Dei. c. 21.

mysteries of the faith, defending them against the
furious onslaughts of their adversaries; at another
he would destroy the fictions of the Academicians
and the Manichaeans and safely lay the foundations
assure the stability of human science; at another,
again, he would investigate the nature, the origin
and the sources of the evils afflicting mankind. He
also wrote many treatises discussing, with the greatest acuteness, the nature of the angels, the soul, the
human mind, the will and its freedom, religion and
the happy life, time and eternity, and the nature,
also, of bodies subject to change. Later came JOHN
DAMASCENE in the East, who followed in the footsteps of Basil and GREGORY of NAZIANZEN; while
BOETHIUS and ANSELM in the West taught the doctrines of Augustine. All three greatly enriched the
patrimony of philosophy.

They were succeeded by the Doctors of the Middle Ages, generally called the SCHOOLMEN. These
undertook the immense task of diligently gathering
together the abundant and fruitful harvests of doctrine scattered in the voluminous writings of the
Holy Fathers, and of laying them up, once gathered,
in one place for the use and convenience of genera-
tions to come. The origin, nature and excellence of
the scholastic philosophy, Venerable Brethren, are
admirably set forth in the words, which it is a pleasure to quote, of a man of pre-eminent wisdom, Our

Predecessor Sixtus V: "By the divine favour of Him Who alone gives the spirit of knowledge and wisdom and understanding and Who enriches His Church throughout the ages, as need arises, with fresh blessings and provides it with fresh assistance, our ancestors, men of profound wisdom, devised the scholastic Theology; which two glorious Doctors especially, the angelic St. Thomas and the seraphic St. Bonaventura, both most illustrious teachers in this faculty . . . cultivated and adorned with surpassing intelligence, devoted application, unceasing labour and unwearying diligence, and transmitted to posterity, arranged in the most admirable order and with most various and illuminating explanations. The knowledge and practical application of this most salutary science, whose principles derive from the abundant sources of Holy Scripture, the acts of the Supreme Pontiffs, the works of the holy Fathers and the decrees of the Councils of the Church, have at all times been of the greatest assistance in enabling the Church to understand exactly and interpret faithfully the text of Scripture, to read and expound the Fathers with greater certainty and profit, to detect and refute errors and heresies; but it is above all in times such as the present, when we are living amid the dangers described by the Apostle, and blasphemous men, exultant and seductive, unceasingly progress in evil, themselves steeped

in error leading others astray, that it is supremely
necessary for confirming the dogmas of the Catholic faith and the refutation of heresies." [30]

Such words would seem to refer only to the theology of the Schoolmen, but it is nevertheless clear
that they are to be taken as applicable also in praise
of their philosophy. The reason is that the eminent
qualities which make the scholastic philosophy so
formidable an opponent to the enemies of truth—
namely, as the same Pontiff adds, "that exact and
inter-related coherence between things and their
causes, that order and disposition as of soldiers drawn
up in battle array, those perspicuous definitions and
distinctions, that strength in argument and subtlety
in controversy whereby light is distinguished from
darkness and truth from error and the wrapping of
deceit and sophism is torn off, like a garment, from
the lies of heretics so that they are stripped bare and
their nakedness exposed" [31]—all those eminent and
admirable qualities are to be attributed solely to a
proper use of that philosophy which the Masters of
the Schools had carefully and deliberately adopted
even in theological disputations. Moreover, it is the
peculiar and distinctive characteristic of Scholastic
theologians to associate human science and divine in

[30] Bull *Triumphantis* (1588).
[31] Bull *Triumphantis*.

the closest possible bond; and theology, in which they excelled, would certainly never have secured so much honour and reputation in the general estimation, if they had made use of a defective or imperfect or superficial philosophy.

Now above all the Doctors of the Schools towers the figure of THOMAS AQUINAS, the leader and master of them all, who, as Cajetan observes, "because he had the utmost reverence for the Doctors of antiquity, seems to have inherited in a way the intellect of all." [32] Thomas gathered their doctrines together—they had long lain dispersed like the scattered limbs of a body—and knitted them into one whole. He disposed them in marvellous order and increased them to such an extent that he is rightly and deservedly considered the pre-eminent guardian and glory of the Catholic Church. His mind was at once docile and penetrating, his memory quick and retentive, the character of his life irreproachable, his devotion to truth single and unqualified, his learning in things human and divine superabundant. He may be compared to the sun, for he warmed the world with the warmth of his virtues and filled it with the radiance of his teaching. There is no branch of philosophy which he did not treat with as much acumen as thoroughness; his discussions of the laws

[32] *In* II–II, 148, 4, *in finem.*

247

of reasoning, God and incorporeal substances, man and the rest of the sensible creation, human conduct and the principles governing it, are so exhaustive that there is nothing lacking in his teaching. It embraces a fruitful crop of topics, an appropriate disposition of parts, perfection of method, firmness of principle, cogency of argument, clarity of exposition, propriety of expression, and facility in the explanation of every abstruse point.

The Angelic Doctor, moreover, considered philosophical conclusions in the reasons and principles of things, which, as they are infinite in extent, so also contain the seeds of almost infinite truths for succeeding masters to cultivate in the appropriate season and bring forth an abundant harvest of fruit. The application of this method of philosophy to the refutation of errors achieved a double success in that it both triumphed unaided over all the errors of preceding ages and provided an arsenal of invincible weapons for routing such as are inevitably bound to arise in future. Again, beginning by establishing, as is only proper, the distinction between reason and faith, while still linking each to the other in a bond of friendly harmony, he maintained the legitimate rights of both, and preserved their respective dignities in such a way that human reason soared to the loftiest heights on the wings of Thomas and can scarcely rise any higher, while faith can expect no further or more reliable assistance than such as it has already received from Thomas.

For these reasons learned men of the highest eminence in theology and philosophy in preceding ages more particularly eagerly sought the immortal works of Thomas and devoted themselves, not so much to cultivating the angelic wisdom, as to soaking themselves in its principles.

It is notorious that nearly all the founders and lawgivers of religious Orders made it compulsory for their brethren to devote themselves, and religiously to adhere, to the doctrines of St. Thomas and forbade them to depart in the slightest degree from the path traced by so illustrious a man. Not to mention the Dominican family, which boasts this consummate master as one of its own special glories, their respective statutes testify that Benedictines, Carmelites, Augustinians, the Society of Jesus and many other religious Orders are bound by the same law.

In this connexion the mind dwells gladly upon those celebrated schools and academies which were once so flourishing in Europe, the Universities of Paris, Salamanca, Alcolà, Douai, Toulouse, Louvain, Padua, Bologna, Naples, Coimbra and numerous other cities. Everybody knows that the reputation of these schools increased with time, that their opinion was solicited in matters of the gravest moment and universally held in the highest esteem. It is also the fact that St. Thomas sat enthroned, like a prince in his kingdom, in all those great houses of human wisdom and that the minds of all, even the Doctors, reposed with marvellous unanimity upon the teaching and authority of the one Angelic Doctor.

What is even more important, the Roman Pontiffs, Our Predecessors, bestowed the most singular commendation and the most lavish testimonials on the wisdom of Thomas Aquinas.

Clement VI in the Bull *In ordine,* Nicholas V in his Brief to the Friars of the Order of Preachers, 1451, Benedict XIII in the Bull *Pretiosus,* and others, testify to the lustre shed upon the universal Church by his admirable doctrine; St. Pius V, indeed, declares in the Bull *Mirabilis* that heresies are confounded, convicted and dissipated by this same philosophy and the world daily delivered from pestiferous errors; others, such as Clement XII in the Bull *Verbo Dei,* that his writings have conferred the most fruitful blessings upon the universal Church and that he is to be accorded the same respect as is paid to the supreme Doctors of the Church, to Gregory, Ambrose, Augustine and Jerome. Others again have had no hesitation in proposing St. Thomas as a model and master whom academies and colleges could safely follow. The words which the Blessed Urban V addressed to the Academy of Toulouse may fittingly be recalled in the context: "We desire and bid you by these presents to follow the doctrine of the Blessed Thomas as truthful and Catholic and to strive with all your strength to develop it." [33] The example of Urban V was followed by Innocent XII in the Letter in the form of a Brief addressed on the 6th February, 1694, to the University of Louvain, and by Benedict XIV in the Letter in the form of a Brief addressed on the 26th August, 1752, to the Dionysian College of Granada. The testimony of Innocent VI, however, may be considered the summary of all the judgments pronounced by the Supreme Pontiffs on Thomas Aquinas: "His doctrine exceeds all others, with the exception of canon law, in propriety of expression, precision of definition and truth of statement, so that those who have once grasped it are never found to have deviated far from the path of truth; and anyone impugning it has always been held suspect of error." [34]

The Oecumenical Councils, also, so distinguished by the presence of an élite of wisdom chosen from the whole world, have always been zealous to pay particular honour to Thomas Aquinas. He may be said to have taken part in, nay, to have presided at, the deliberations and the decrees of the Fathers at

[33] *Cons. V. ad Cancell. Univ. Tolos.*, 1368.
[34] *Sermo de S. Thoma.*

the Councils of Lyons, Vienne, Florence and the Vatican, and to have combated with invincible energy and the happiest success the errors of Greeks, heretics and rationalists. The greatest honour ever paid to St. Thomas, however, an honour never before accorded to any Catholic Doctor, is that the Fathers of Trent decreed that during their sessions the *Summa* of Thomas Aquinas should be laid open on the altar with the books of Holy Scripture and the decrees of the Supreme Pontiffs for them to resort to it in case of need for counsel, arguments and oracles.

Lastly, this laurel also seems to have been reserved for this incomparable man that he was able to wring respect, praise and admiration even from the enemies of the Catholic name. For it is well known that many leaders of heretical factions have openly declared that, if the philosophy of Thomas Aquinas were once disposed of, they could easily "engage in the contest with and vanquish all the Catholic doctors," and "scatter the Church." [35] It was an idle hope, to be sure, but not an idle testimony.

For all these reasons, Venerable Brethren, when We consider the virtue and efficacy of, and the exceptional advantages to be derived from, a philosophy held in such high estimation by our ancestors, We think that it was a foolish omission not to con-

[35] Theodore Beza (de Bèze) and Martin Bucer.

tinue to pay it always and everywhere the honour it deserves, especially as it was plain that the Scholastic philosophy had in its favour long experience, the approbation of the most eminent men and—which is also of high importance—the commendation of the Church. A new system of philosophy, however, has been introduced here and there in place of the ancient doctrine and yet has not produced such desirable and wholesome fruit as the Church and civil society itself would have preferred. Under the influence of the Reformers of the sixteenth century, men began to philosophize in complete disregard of the faith, taking and granting the liberty of thinking whatever his caprice and inclination suggested to each. The natural consequence was the multiplication of philosophical systems beyond all reason, and the emergence of the most various and contradictory opinions even with regard to things of the utmost importance in human knowledge. The multitude of opinions in many cases produced hesitation and doubt; and anyone can see how easily men's minds slip from doubt into error.

Example is catching and the passion for novelty seemed to have affected the minds of Catholic philosophers also in some places. They began to look down upon their inheritance of ancient wisdom and preferred to build anew rather than to augment and perfect the old by the new; it was undoubtedly an imprudent project and it did harm to the sciences. For these innumerable systems, being based upon the shifting foundation of the authority and judgment of the individual philosopher, were incapable of producing as solid and stable and substantial a philosophy as the old, and the result was an unstable and inconsistent one. If such a philosophy, therefore, should one day find itself powerless to repel the enemy's attack, it will be forced to admit that the cause and fault thereof reside in itself alone. In so saying, We are far from reproaching those learned and skilful men who devote their industry and erudition and all the wealth of new inventions to the development of philosophy. We realize perfectly that their labours assist the progress of science. But the greatest care should be taken not to make such industry or erudition the whole or the principal end of philosophy. The same consideration applies to sacred theology; it is right to support and illuminate it with copious learning but it is absolutely essential that it be treated according to the severe custom of the Schoolmen, so that, combining the strength of revelation and reason, it may continue to be the inexpugnable bulwark of faith.[36]

They were therefore very happily inspired— those numerous devotees of the philosophical sci-

[36] Sixtus V, Bull *cit.*

ences who in a recent attempt usefully to restore
philosophy, endeavoured and continue their en-
deavours to revive the excellent philosophy of
Thomas Aquinas and to re-establish it in the esteem
in which it was once held. It was a great joy to Us,
Venerable Brethren, to learn that members of your
Order, animated by a like desire, had eagerly embarked on the same course. We heartily commend
their undertaking and encourage them to persevere
in their design. We warn you, each and everyone,
that there is nothing We have so long and so earnestly
desired as that you all offer generously and copiously
to youth engaged in studies the limpid streams of
wisdom which flow from the Angelic Doctor as from
an abundant, inexhaustible spring.

The reasons inspiring Us with this ardent desire
are many. In the first place, considering that the
Christian faith is generally attacked at the present
day by the machinations and subtle devices of every
kind of illusory philosophy, it is essential that all
young men, and those especially whose education is
the hope of the Church, be nourished with the sound
and substantial food of doctrine, so that, valiant in
strength and provided with a plentiful supply of
weapons, they may soon learn to defend the cause of
religion forcibly and prudently, "being ready
always," in accordance with the apostolic precepts,

"to satisfy everyone that asketh a reason of that hope which is in us" [37] and, also, "to exhort in sound doctrine and to convince the gainsayers." [38]

Again, the majority of these whose minds are alienated from truth and who hate Catholic institutions maintain that reason is their sole mistress and guide. To cure them of this delusion and bring them back to favour with the Catholic faith, We consider that next after the supernatural help of God nothing is more apt than the substantial teaching of the Fathers and the Schoolmen. They demonstrate the solid foundations upon which faith reposes, its divine origin and certain truth, the arguments by which a man may be persuaded to accept it, the benefits it has conferred upon the human race and its perfect harmony with reason, all with such a weight of evidence as is amply sufficient to convince even the most obstinate and recalcitrant minds.

There is none of us but can see the danger in which the family and civil society itself are involved owing to the plague of perverse opinions; they would certainly be much more tranquil and secure if a sounder doctrine, one more in conformity with the teaching of the Church, were taught in schools, such a doctrine as is contained in the works of Thomas Aquinas. For the theses which St. Thomas

[37] *I Peter*, iii, 15.
[38] *Titus*, i, 9.

maintains with regard to the true nature of liberty, now degenerated into licence, the divine origin of all authority, laws and the obligation they impose, the just and paternal sovereignty of kings, the obedience due to the higher powers, the necessity of mutual charity among all men and such like, are of supreme and irresistible efficacy in rebutting those principles of the new jurisprudence which appear brimful of menace to the tranquillity of the State and the public safety.

Lastly, all branches of human science may legitimately hope to make progress in reliance upon the assurance of substantial support from such a renovation of philosophy as We propose. For the liberal arts have habitual recourse to philosophy as to controlling wisdom for their supreme regulation and proper method and derive from philosophy as from a common source of life the spirit animating them. The fact is, and constant experience shows, that the liberal arts were ever most flourishing when philosophy preserved its honour intact and its judgment wise; but when philosophy declined and became involved in errors or follies, the liberal arts lay languishing in neglect and were well-nigh abandoned.

The natural sciences themselves, which are held in such high estimation at the present day and everywhere attract through so many magnificent discoveries an admiration without parallel, so far from suffering the least harm, would, on the contrary, derive singular advantage from a restoration of the ancient philosophy. For the mere consideration of facts and the observation of nature are not sufficient for their fruitful exercise and increase; once the facts have been discovered, the scientist must rise to a higher plane and set himself painstakingly to ascertain the nature of corporeal things, must discover the laws which they obey and the principles governing the order which they reveal, the unity in their variety and the mutual affinity in their diversity. Scholastic philosophy, wisely taught, would contribute to such investigations a marvellous increase of energy and a flood of illumination.

It is only right in this connexion to declare that supreme injustice is done to this philosophy by the allegation that it is opposed to the progress and development of the natural sciences. For as the Schoolmen, therein following the common tradition of the holy Fathers, taught at every step in anthropology that the mind cannot raise itself except by sensible things to the knowledge of incorporeal and immaterial things, so they also realized that nothing could be more useful to the philosopher than diligent scrutiny of the secrets of nature and the devotion of much time and care to the study of physical phenomena. They confirmed this theory in their practice; for St. Thomas, the Blessed Albert the Great, and other leaders of the School did not give themselves up so entirely to the study of philosophy as to exclude any attempt to acquire a knowledge of nature, and many of their observations and theories in this sphere have won the approval of modern scientists and are admittedly congruent with truth. Many distinguished professors of the physical sciences at the present time publicly and openly declare that there is no real conflict between the certain and confirmed conclusions of modern physics and the philosophical principles of the School.

Therefore in declaring that every sagacious observation, every useful invention made or devised by anyone, is to be gladly and gratefully welcomed, We earnestly exhort you, Venerable Brethren, for the protection and glory of the Catholic faith, for the welfare of society, for the advancement of all sciences, to restore the precious wisdom of St. Thomas and to propagate it as far as possible. The wisdom of St. Thomas We say: for if there be any proposition too subtly investigated or too inconsiderately taught by the Doctors of the School, any tenet of theirs not strictly in conformity with subsequent discoveries or in any way improbable in itself, it is no part of Our intention to propose that for the imitation of Our time. For the rest, let masters, discriminately chosen by you, devote themselves to inculcating the philosophy of St. Thomas into the minds of their pupils, clearly demonstrating its solidity and value in comparison with other systems. Let the Academies which you have already founded, or which you will found in future, illustrate and cherish that philosophy and make use of it to repel the assaults of error.

Be careful, however, that the wisdom of Thomas be drawn from the spring itself or at any rate from streams which, flowing from that spring, still, in the certain and unanimous opinion of learned men, run pure and undefiled; that no supposititious draught be taken in place of a true, or muddied water instead of the pure; preserve the minds of your young men from streams which, while said to flow from that spring, are in reality swollen with alien and unhealthy matter. We are, however, fully aware that all Our efforts will be in vain, if Our common undertaking, Venerable Brethren, fails to receive the support of Him Who is described in Holy Writ as "a God of all knowledge," [39] as by Scripture also we are told that "every best gift, and every perfect gift, is from above, coming down from the Father of lights," [40] and again, "if any . . . want wisdom, let him ask of God Who giveth

[39] *I Kings*, ii, 3.
[40] *James*, i, 17.

to all men abundantly, and upbraideth not: and it shall be given him." [41]

In this matter also, let us follow the example of the Angelic Doctor who never read or wrote without first propitiating God in prayer; and Who candidly confessed that he had not acquired whatever learning he possessed by his own study and diligence, but had received it from God. Let us therefore humbly supplicate God together to inspire the sons of the Church with the spirit of knowledge and understanding and to open their minds to the perception of wisdom. That the fruits of the divine goodness may descend upon you in greater abundance, solicit also the most powerful advocacy before the throne of God of the Blessed Virgin Mary, who is called the Seat of Wisdom, and have recourse at the same time to the intervention of the Blessed Joseph, the most chaste spouse of the Blessed Virgin, and to Peter and Paul, the princes of the Apostles who by truth renewed a world, which had grown corrupt through the contagion of errors, and filled it full of the light of the heavenly wisdom.

Lastly, in reliance upon the hope of the divine assistance and trusting to your pastoral zeal, We most affectionately give to every one of you, Venerable Brethren, and to all the clergy and people severally committed to your care, Our Apostolic

[41] *Ibid.,* i, 5.

blessing in the Lord and may it be an earnest to you of the favour of Heaven, as it is a testimony of the love We bear you.

Given at Rome, at St. Peter's, on the 4th day of August, 1879, in the second year of Our Pontificate.

Leo PP. XIII.

II

DOCTORIS ANGELICI

Motu proprio for Italy and the adjacent islands, to encourage the study of the philosophy of St. Thomas Aquinas in Catholic Schools.

No true Catholic has ever ventured to call in question the opinion of the Angelic Doctor that: The regulation of studies is the special concern of the authority of the Holy See by which the universal Church is governed and the need is met by the establishment of Universities (Opusc. *Contra impugnantes Dei cultum et religionem,* iii). We have already discharged this great duty of Our office elsewhere, and more particularly on the 1st September, 1910, when in the Letter *Sacrorum Antistitum,* addressed to all Bishops and Superiors of Religious Orders duly charged with the duty of educating young men for the priesthood, We counselled them in the first place as follows: "So far as studies are concerned, it is Our will and We hereby explicitly ordain that the Scholastic philosophy be considered as the basis of sacred studies. . . . And what is of capital importance in prescribing that Scholastic philosophy is to be followed, We have in mind particularly the philosophy which has been transmitted to us by St. Thomas Aquinas. It is Our desire that all the enactments of Our Predecessor in respect thereto be maintained in full force; and, where need be, We renew and conform them and order them to be strictly observed by all concerned. Let Bishops urge and compel their observance in future in any Seminary in which they may have been neglected. The same injunction applies also to Superiors of Religious Orders."

Now because the word We used in the text of that letter recommending the philosophy of Aquinas was "particularly," and not "exclusively," certain persons persuaded themselves that they were acting in conformity to Our Will or at any rate not actively opposing it, in adopting indiscriminately and adhering to the philosophical opinions of any other Doctor of the School, even though such opinions were contrary to the principles of St. Thomas. They were greatly deceived. In recommending St. Thomas to Our subjects as supreme guide in the Scholastic philosophy, it goes without saying that Our intention was to be understood as referring above all to those principles upon which that philosophy is based as its foundation. For just as the opinion of certain ancients is to be rejected which maintains that it makes no difference to the truth of the Faith what any man thinks about the nature of creation, provided his opinions on the nature of God be sound, because error with regard to the nature of creation begets a false knowledge of God; so the principles of philosophy laid down by St. Thomas Aquinas are to be religiously and inviolably observed, because they are the means of acquiring such a knowledge of creation as is most congruent with the Faith (*Contra Gentiles,* ii, 2, 3); of refuting all the errors of all the ages, and of enabling man to distinguish clearly what things are to be attributed to God and to God alone (*ibid.,* iii; and *Sum. Theol.,* I, xii, 4; and liv, 1). They also marvellously illustrate the diversity and analogy between God and His works, a diversity and analogy admirably expressed by the Fourth Lateran Council as follows: "The resemblance between the Creator and the creature is such that their still greater dissimilarity cannot fail to be observed" (*Decretalis* iii, *Damnamus ergo,* etc. Cf. St. Thomas, *Quaest. disp. De Scientia Dei,* ii).—For the rest, the principles of St. Thomas, considered generally and as a whole, contain nothing but what the most eminent philosophers and doctors of the Church have discovered after prolonged reflection and discussion in regard to the particular reasons determining human knowledge, the nature of God and creation, the moral order and the ultimate end to be pursued in life.

St. Thomas perfected and augmented still further by the almost angelic quality of his intellect all this superb patrimony of wisdom which he inherited from his predecessors and applied it to prepare, illustrate and protect sacred doctrine in the minds of men (*In Librum Boethii de Trinitate, quaest.* ii, 3). Sound reason suggests that it would be foolish to neglect it and religion will not suffer it to be in any way attenuated. And rightly, because, if Catholic doctrine is once deprived of this strong bulwark, it is useless to seek the slightest assistance for its defence in a philosophy whose principles are either common to the errors of materialism, monism, pantheism, socialism and modernism, or certainly not opposed to such systems. The reason is that the capital theses in the philosophy of St. Thomas are not to be placed in the category of opinions capable of being debated one way or another, but are to be considered as the foundations upon which the whole science of natural and divine things is based; if such principles are once removed or in any way impaired, it must necessarily follow that students of the sacred sciences will ultimately fail to perceive so much as the meaning of the words in which the dogmas of divine revelation are proposed by the magistracy of the Church.

We therefore desired that all teachers of philosophy and sacred theology should be warned that if they deviated so much as a step, in metaphysics especially, from Aquinas, they exposed themselves to grave risk.—We now go further and solemnly declare that those who in their interpretations misrepresent or affect to despise the principles and major theses of his philosophy are not only not following St. Thomas but are even far astray from the saintly Doctor. If the doctrine of any writer or Saint has ever been approved by Us or Our Predecessors with such singular commendation and in such a way that to the commendation were added an invitation and order to propagate and defend it, it may easily be understood that it was commended to the extent that it agreed with the principles of Aquinas or was in no way opposed to them.

We have deemed it Our apostolic duty to make this declaration and order so that the clergy, both regular and secular, may clearly know Our will and mind in a matter of the gravest importance, and fulfil Our desire with the appropriate alacrity and diligence. Teachers of Christian philosophy and sacred theology will be particularly zealous in this respect, for they must bear in mind that they have not been entrusted with the duty of teaching in order to impart to their pupils whatever opinions they please, but to instruct them in the most approved doctrines of the Church.

As for sacred theology itself, it is Our desire that the study of it be always illuminated by the light of the philosophy before referred to, but in ordinary clerical seminaries, provided suitable teachers are available, there is no objection to the use of text books containing summaries of doctrines derived from the source of Aquinas. There is an ample supply of excellent works of the kind.

But for the more profound study of this science, as it ought to be studied in Universities and Colleges and in all Seminaries and Institutions which are empowered to grant academic degrees, it is of the first importance that the old system of lecturing on the actual text of the *Summa Theologica*—which should never have been allowed to fall into disuse—be revived; for the reason also that prelections on this book make it easier to understand and to illustrate the solemn decrees of the teaching Church and the acts passed in consequence. For ever since the happy death of the saintly Doctor, the Church has not held a single Council, but he has been present at it with the wealth of his doctrine. The experience of so many centuries has shown and every passing day more clearly proves the truth of the statement made by Our Predecessor

John XXII: "He (Thomas Aquinas) enlightened the Church more than all the other Doctors together; a man can derive more profit from his books in one year than from a lifetime spent in pondering the philosophy of others" (Consistorial address of 1318). St. Pius V confirmed this opinion when he ordered the feast of St. Thomas as Doctor to be kept by the universal Church: "But inasmuch as, by the providence of Almighty God, the power and truth of the philosophy of the Angelic Doctor, ever since his enrolment amongst the citizens of Heaven, have confounded, refuted and routed many subsequent heresies, as was so often clearly seen in the past and was lately apparent in the sacred decrees of the Council of Trent, We order that the memory of the Doctor by whose valour the world is daily delivered from pestilential errors be cultivated more than ever before with feelings of pious and grateful devotion" (Bull *Mirabilis Deus* of the 11th April, 1567). To avoid recapitulating the many other resounding praises of Our Predecessors, We may adopt the following words of Benedict XIV as a summary of all the commendations bestowed upon the writings of Thomas Aquinas, more particularly the *Summa Theologica:* "Numerous Roman Pontiffs, Our Predecessors, have borne glorious testimony to his philosophy. We, also, in the books which We have written on various topics, after by diligent examination perceiving and considering the mind of the Angelic Doctor, have always adhered and subscribed with joy and admiration to his philosophy, and candidly confess that whatever good is to be found in Our own Writings is in no way to be attributed to Us, but entirely to so eminent a teacher (*Acta Cap. Gen. O.P., vol. XI*, p. 196).

Therefore that "the philosophy of St. Thomas may flourish incorrupt and entire in schools, which is very dear to Our heart," and that "the system of teaching which is based upon the authority and judgment of the individual teacher" and therefore "has a changeable foundation whence many diverse and mutually conflicting opinions arise . . . not without great injury to Christian learning" (Leo XIII, *Epist. Qui te* of the 19th June, 1886) be abolished forever, it is Our will and We hereby order and command that teachers of sacred theology in Universities, Academies, Colleges, Seminaries and Institutions enjoying by apostolic indult the privilege of granting academatic degrees and doctorates in philosophy, use the *Summa Theologica* of St. Thomas as the text of their prelections and comment upon it in the Latin tongue, and let them take particular care to inspire their pupils with a devotion for it.

Such is already the laudable custom of many In-

stitutions. Such was the rule which the sagacious
founders of Religious Orders, with the hearty approval of Our Predecessors, desired should be observed in their own houses of study; and the saintly
men who came after the time of St. Thomas
Aquinas took him and no other for their supreme
teacher of philosophy. So also and not otherwise
will theology recover its pristine glory and all sacred studies be restored to their order and value and
the province of the intellect and reason flower again
in a second spring.

In future, therefore, no power to grant academic
degrees in sacred theology will be given to any in-
stitution unless Our present prescription is religiously observed therein. Institutions or Faculties
of Orders and Regular Congregations, also, already
in lawful possession of the power of conferring
such academic degrees or similar diplomas, even
within the limits of their own four walls, shall be
deprived of such a privilege and be considered to
have been so deprived if, after the lapse of three
years, they shall not have religiously obeyed for any
reason whatsoever, even beyond their control, this
Our injunction.

This is Our Order, and nothing shall be suffered
to gainsay it.

Given at Rome, at St. Peter's, on the 29th day of

June, 1914, the eleventh year of Our Pontificate.

Pius PP. X.

III

STUDIORUM DUCEM

ENCYCLICAL LETTER OF OUR MOST HOLY LORD
POPE PIUS XI, ON THE OCCASION OF THE SIXTH
CENTENARY OF THE CANONIZATION OF THOMAS
AQUINAS

To Our Venerable Brethren,
the Patriarchs, Primates, Archbishops, Bishops
and other Ordinaries
in grace and communion with the Apostolic See
Pius XI, Pope
Venerable Brethren,
Greeting and the Apostolic Benediction:

IN a recent apostolic letter confirming the statutes of Canon Law, We declared that the guide to be followed in the higher studies by young men training for the priesthood was Thomas Aquinas. The approaching anniversary of the day when he was duly enrolled, six hundred years ago, in the calendar of the Saints, offers Us an admirable opportunity of

271

inculcating this more and more firmly in the minds of Our students and explaining to them what advantage they may most usefully derive from the teaching of so illustrious a Doctor. For science truly deserving of the name and piety, the companion of all the virtues, are related in a marvellous bond of affinity, and, as God is very Truth and very Goodness, it would assuredly not be sufficient to procure the glory of God by the salvation of souls—the chief task and peculiar mission of the Church—if ministers of religion were well disciplined in knowledge and not also abundantly provided at the same time with the appropriate virtues.

Such a combination of doctrine and piety, of erudition and virtue, of truth and charity, is to be found in an eminent degree in the Angelic Doctor and it is not without reason that he has been given the sun for a device; for he both brings the light of learning into the minds of men and fires their hearts and wills with the virtues. God, the Source of all sanctity and wisdom would, therefore, seem to have desired to show in the case of Thomas how each of these qualities assists the other, how the practice of the virtues disposes to the contemplation of truth, and the profound consideration of truth in turn gives lustre and perfection to the virtues. For the man of pure and upright life, whose passions are controlled by virtue, is delivered as it

were of a heavy burden and can much more easily raise his mind to heavenly things and penetrate more profoundly into the secrets of God, according to the maxim of Thomas himself: "Life comes before learning: for life leads to the knowledge of truth" (*Comment. in Matth.*, v); and if such a man devotes himself to the investigation of the supernatural, he will find a powerful incentive in such a pursuit to lead a perfect life; for the learning of such sublime things, the beauty of which is a ravishing ecstasy, so far from being a solitary or sterile occupation, must be said to be on the contrary most practical.

These are among the first lessons, Venerable Brethren, which may be learned from the commemoration of this centenary; but that they may be the more clearly apparent, We propose to comment briefly in this Letter on the sanctity and doctrine of Thomas Aquinas and to show what profitable instruction may be derived therefrom by priests, by seminarians especially, and, not least, by all Christian people.

Thomas possessed all the moral virtues to a very high degree and so closely bound together that, as he himself insists should be the case, they formed one whole in charity "which informs the acts of all the virtues" (II–II, xxiii, 8; I–II, lxv). If, however, we seek to discover the peculiar and specific char-

acteristics of his sanctity, there occurs to Us in the
first place that virtue which gives Thomas a certain
likeness to the angelic natures, and that is chastity;
he preserved it unsullied in a crisis of the most pressing danger and was therefore considered worthy to
be surrounded by the angels with a mystic girdle.
This perfect regard for purity was accompanied at
the same time by an equal aversion for fleeting possessions and a contempt for honours; it is recorded
that his firmness of purpose overcame the obstinate
persistence of relatives who strove their utmost to
induce him to accept a lucrative situation in the
world and that later, when the Supreme Pontiff
would have offered him a mitre, his prayers were
successful in securing that such a dread burden
should not be laid upon him. The most distinctive
feature, however, of the sanctity of Thomas is what
St. Paul describes as the "word of wisdom" (I *Cor.*
xii, 8) and that combination of the two forms of
wisdom, the acquired and the infused, as they are
termed, with which nothing accords so well as humility, devotion to prayer, and the love of God.

That humility was the foundation upon which
the other virtues of Thomas were based is clear to
anyone who considers how submissively he obeyed
a lay brother in the course of their communal life;
and it is no less patent to anyone reading his writings which manifest such respect for the Fathers of

the Church that "because he had the utmost reverence for the doctors of antiquity, he seems to have inherited in a way the intellect of all" (Leo XIII, *ex Card. Caietano, litt. Encycl. Aeterni Patris,* 4th August, 1879); but the most magnificent illustration of it is to be found in the fact that he devoted the faculties of his divine intellect not in the least to gain glory for himself, but to the advancement of truth. Most philosophers as a rule are eager to establish their own reputations, but Thomas strove to efface himself completely in the teaching of his philosophy so that the light of heavenly truth might shine with its own effulgence.

This humility, therefore, combined with the purity of heart We have mentioned, and sedulous devotion to prayer, disposed the mind of Thomas to docility in receiving the inspirations of the Holy Ghost and following His illuminations, which are the first principles of contemplation. To obtain them from above, he would frequently fast, spend whole nights in prayer, lean his head in the fervour of his unaffected piety against the tabernacle containing the august Sacrament, constantly turn his eyes and mind in sorrow to the image of the crucified Jesus; and he confessed to his intimate friend St. Bonaventura that it was from that Book especially that he derived all his learning. It may, therefore, be truly said of Thomas what is commonly re-

ported of St. Dominic, Father and Lawgiver, that in his conversation he never spoke but about God or with God.

But as he was accustomed to contemplate all things in God, the first Cause and ultimate End of all things, it was easy for him to follow in his *Summa Theologica* no less than in his life the two kinds of wisdom before referred to. He himself describes them as follows: "The wisdom which is acquired by human effort . . . gives a man a sound judgement with regard to divine things according as he makes a perfect use of reason. . . . But there is another kind of wisdom which comes down from above . . . and judges divine things in virtue of a certain connaturality with them. This wisdom is the gift of the Holy Ghost . . . and through it a man becomes perfect in divine things, not only by learning but also by experiencing divine things" (II–II, xlv, 1, ad 2; 2).

This wisdom, therefore, which comes down from, or is infused by, God, accompanied by the other gifts of the Holy Ghost, continually grew and increased in Thomas, along with charity, the mistress and queen of all the virtues. Indeed it was an absolutely certain doctrine of his that the love of God should ever continually increase "in accordance with the very words of the commandment: 'Thou shalt love the Lord, thy God, with thy whole

heart'; for the whole and the perfect are one same thing. . . . Now the end of the commandment is charity from a pure heart, and a good conscience and an unfeigned faith, as the Apostle says (I *Tim.* i, 5), but no standard of measure is applicable to the end, but only to such things as conduce to the end (II–II, clxxxiv, 3)." This is the very reason why the perfection of charity falls under the commandment as the end to which we ought all to strive, each according to his degree. Moreover, as "it is the characteristic of charity to make man tend to God by uniting the affections of man to God in such a way that man ceases to live for himself and lives only for God" (II–II, xvii, 6, ad 3), so the love of God, continually increasing in Thomas along with that double wisdom, induced in him in the end such absolute forgetfulness of self that when Jesus spoke to him from the cross, saying: "Thomas, thou hast written well about me," and asked him: "What reward shall I give thee for all thy labour?" the saint made answer: "None but Thyself, O Lord!" Instinct with charity, therefore, he unceasingly continued to serve the convenience of others, not counting the cost, by writing admirable books, helping his brethren in their labours, depriving himself of his own garments to give them to the poor, even restoring the sick to health as, for example, when preaching in the Vatican Basilica

277

on the occasion of the Easter celebrations, he suddenly cured a woman who had touched the hem of his habit of a chronic hæmorrhage.

In what other Doctor was this "word of wisdom" mentioned by St. Paul more remarkable and abundant than in the Angelic Doctor? He was not satisfied with enlightening the minds of men by his teaching: he exerted himself strenuously to rouse their hearts to make a return of His love to God, the Creator of all things. "The love of God is the source and origin of goodness in things" he magnificently declares (I, xx, 2), and he ceaselessly illustrates this diffusion of the divine goodness in his discussion of every several mystery. "Hence it is of the nature of perfect good to communicate itself in a perfect way and this is done in a supreme degree by God . . . in the Incarnation" (III, i, 1). Nothing, however, shows the force of his genius and charity so clearly as the Office which he himself composed for the august Sacrament. The words he uttered on his death-bed, as he was about to receive the holy Viaticum, are the measure of his devotion to that Sacrament throughout his life: "I receive Thee, Price of the redemption of my soul, for the love of Whom I have studied, kept vigil and toiled."

After this slight sketch of the great virtues of Thomas, it is easy to understand the pre-eminence

of his doctrine and the marvellous authority it enjoys in the Church. Our Predecessors, indeed, have always unanimously extolled it. Even during the lifetime of the saint, Alexander IV had no hesitation in addressing him in these terms: "To Our beloved son, Thomas Aquinas, distinguished alike for nobility of blood and integrity of character, who has acquired by the grace of God the treasure of divine and human learning." After his death, again, John XXII seemed to consecrate both his virtues and his doctrine when, addressing the Cardinals, he uttered in full Consistory the memorable sentence: "He alone enlightened the Church more than all other doctors; a man can derive more profit in a year from his books than from pondering all his life the teaching of others."

He enjoyed a more than human reputation for intellect and learning and Pius V was therefore moved to enroll him officially among the holy Doctors with the title of *Angelic*. Again, could there be any more manifest indication of the very high esteem in which this Doctor is held by the Church than the fact that the Fathers of Trent resolved that two volumes only, Holy Scripture and the *Summa Theologica*, should be reverently laid open on the altar during their deliberations? And in this order of ideas, to avoid recapitulating the innumerable testimonies of the Apostolic See, We are happy

to recall that the philosophy of Aquinas was revived by the authority and at the instance of Leo XIII; the merit of Our illustrious Predecessor in so doing is such, as We have said elsewhere, that if he had not been the author of many acts and decrees of surpassing wisdom, this alone would be sufficient to establish his undying glory. Pope Pius X of saintly memory followed shortly afterwards in his footsteps, more particularly in his Motu Proprio *Doctoris Angelici*, in which this memorable phrase occurs: "For ever since the happy death of the Doctor, the Church has not held a single Council but he has been present at it with all the wealth of his doctrine." Closer to Us, Our greatly regretted Predecessor Benedict XV repeatedly declared that he was entirely of the same opinion and he is to be praised for having promulgated the Code of Canon Law in which "the system, philosophy and principles of the Angelic Doctor" are unreservedly sanctioned. We so heartily approve the magnificent tribute of praise bestowed upon this most divine genius that We consider that Thomas should be called not only the Angelic, but also the *Common* or Universal Doctor of the Church; for the Church has adopted his philosophy for her own, as innumerable documents of every kind attest. It would be an endless task to explain here all the reasons which moved Our Predecessors in this re-

spect, and it will be sufficient perhaps to point out that Thomas wrote under the inspiration of the supernatural spirit which animated his life and that his writings, which contain the principles of, and the laws governing, all sacred studies, must be said to possess a universal character.

In dealing orally or in writing with divine things, he provides theologians with a striking example of the intimate connexion which should exist between the spiritual and the intellectual life. For just as a man cannot really be said to know some distant country, if his acquaintance is confined merely to a description of it, however accurate, but must have dwelt in it for some little time; so nobody can attain to an intimate knowledge of God by mere scientific investigation, unless he also dwells in the most intimate association with God. The aim of the whole theology of St. Thomas is to bring us into close living intimacy with God. For even as in his childhood at Monte Cassino he unceasingly put the question: "What is God?"; so all the books he wrote concerning the creation of the world, the nature of man, laws, the virtues, and the Sacraments, are all concerned with God, the Author of eternal salvation.

Again, discussing the causes of the sterility of such studies, namely curiosity, that is to say the unbridled desire for knowledge, indolence of mind, aversion from effort and lack of perseverance, he insists that there is no other remedy than zeal in work with the fervour of piety which derives from the life of the spirit. Sacred studies, therefore, being directed by a triple light, undeviating reason, infused faith and the gifts of the Holy Ghost, by which the mind is brought to perfection, no one ever was more generously endowed with these than Our Saint. After spending all the riches of his intellect on some matter of exceptional difficulty, he would seek the solution of his problem from God by the most humble prayer and fasting; and God was wont to listen to His suppliant so kindly that He dispatched the Princes of the Apostles at times to instruct him. It is not therefore surprising that towards the end of his life he had risen to such a degree of contemplation as to declare that all he had written seemed to him mere chaff and that he was incapable of dictating another word; his eyes even then were fixed on eternity alone, his one desire was to see God. For, according to Thomas, by far the most important benefit to be derived from sacred studies, is that they inspire a man with a great love for God and a great longing for eternal things.

He not only instructs us by his example how to pursue such a diversity of studies, but also teaches us firm and enduring principles of each single science. For, in the first place, who has provided a better explanation than he of the nature and character of philosophy, its various divisions and the relative importance of each? Consider how clearly he demonstrates the congruence and harmony between all the various sections which go to make up the body as it were of this science. "It is the function of the wise man," he declares, "to put things in order, because wisdom is primarily the perfection of reason and it is the characteristic of reason to know order; for although the sensitive faculties know some things absolutely, only the intellect or reason can know the relation one thing bears to another. The sciences, therefore, vary according to the various forms of order which reason perceives to be peculiar to each. The order which the consideration of reason establishes in its own peculiar activity pertains to rational philosophy or logic, whose function is to consider the order of the parts of speech in their mutual relations and in relation to the conclusions which may be drawn from them. It is for natural philosophy or physics to consider the order in things which human reason considers but does not itself institute, so that under natural philosophy we include also metaphysics. But the order of voluntary acts is for the consideration of moral philosophy which is divided into three sections: the first considers the activities of the individual man in relation to their end and is called 'monastics'; the second considers the activities of the family group or community and is called economics; the third considers the activities of the State and is called politics" (*Ethics*, I, 1). Thomas dealt thoroughly with all these several divisions of philosophy, each according to its appropriate method, and, beginning with things nearest to our human reason, rose step by step to things more remote until he stood in the end on "the topmost peak of all things" (*Contra Gentes*, II, lvi; IV, i).

His teaching with regard to the power or value of the human mind is irrefragable. "The human mind has a natural knowledge of being and the things which are in themselves part of being as such, and this knowledge is the foundation of our knowledge of first principles" (*Contra Gentes*, II, lxxxiii). Such a doctrine goes to the root of the errors and opinions of those modern philosophers who maintain that it is not being itself which is perceived in the act of intellection, but some modification of the percipient; the logical consequence of such errors is *agnosticism*, which was so vigorously condemned in the Encyclical *Pascendi*.

The arguments adduced by St. Thomas to prove the existence of God and that God alone is subsisting Being Itself are still to-day, as they were in the Middle Ages, the most cogent of all arguments and clearly confirm that dogma of the Church which was solemnly proclaimed at the Vatican Council and succinctly expressed by Pius X as follows: "The certain knowledge of God as the first principle of creation and its end and demonstrable proof of His existence can be inferred, like the knowledge of a cause from its effect, by the light of the natural reason, from creation, that is to say the visible works of creation" (Motu Proprio *Sacrorum Antistitum* of the 1st September, 1910). The metaphysical philosophy of St. Thomas, although exposed to this day to the bitter onslaughts of prejudiced critics, yet still retains, like gold which no acid can dissolve, its full force and splendour unimpaired. Our Predecessor therefore rightly observed: "To deviate from Aquinas, in metaphysics especially, is to run grave risk" (Encycl. *Pascendi* of the 8th September, 1907).

Philosophy is undoubtedly a most noble science, but as things are now constituted by divine Providence, it must not be said to excel all others, because it does not embrace the whole universality of things. Indeed, in the introduction to his *Summa Contra Gentes*, as also to his *Summa Theologica*, the saintly Doctor describes another order of things set above nature and eluding the grasp of reason, an order which man would never have suspected unless the divine goodness had revealed it to him. This is the region in which faith is supreme, and the science of faith is called Theology. Science of this kind will be all the more perfect in a man in proportion as he is the better acquainted with the evidence for faith and has at the same time a more fully developed and trained faculty of philosophizing. There can be no doubt that Aquinas raised Theology to the highest eminence, for his knowledge of divine things was absolutely perfect and the power of his mind made him a marvellously capable philosopher. Thomas is therefore considered the Prince of teachers in our schools, not so much on account of his philosophical system as because of his theological studies. There is no branch of theology in which he did not exercise the incredible fecundity of his genius.

For in the first place he established apologetics on a sound and genuine basis by defining exactly the difference between the province of reason and the province of faith and carefully distinguishing the natural and the supernatural orders. When the sacred Vatican Council, therefore, in determining what natural knowledge of religion was possible, affirmed the relative necessity of some divine revelation for sure and certain knowledge and the absolute necessity of divine revelation for knowledge of the mysteries, it employed arguments which were borrowed precisely from St. Thomas. He insists that all who undertake to defend the Christian faith shall hold sacrosanct the principle that: "It is not mere folly to assent to the things of faith although they are beyond reason" (*Contra Gentes*, I, vi). He shows that, although the articles of belief are mysterious and obscure, the reasons which persuade us to believe are nevertheless clear and perspicuous, for, says he, "a man would not believe unless he saw that there were things to be believed" (II–II, i, 4); and he adds that, so far from being considered a hindrance or a servile yoke imposed upon men, faith should, on the contrary, be reckoned a very great blessing, because "faith in us is a sort of beginning of eternal life" (*Qq. disp. de Veritate*, xiv, 2).

The other branch of Theology, which is concerned with the interpretation of dogmas, also found in St. Thomas by far the richest of all commentators; for nobody ever more profoundly penetrated or expounded with greater subtlety all the august mysteries, as, for example, the intimate life of God, the obscurity of eternal predestination, the supernatural government of the world, the faculty granted to rational creatures of attaining their end, the redemption of the human race achieved by Jesus Christ and continued by the

Church and the sacraments, both of which the Angelic Doctor describes as "relics, so to speak, of the divine Incarnation."

He also composed a substantial moral theology, capable of directing all human acts in accordance with the supernatural last end of man. And as he is, as We have said, the perfect theologian, so he gives infallible rules and precepts of life not only for individuals, but also for civil and domestic society which is the object also of moral science, both economic and politic. Hence those superb chapters in the second part of the *Summa Theologica* on paternal or domestic government, the lawful power of the State or the nation, natural and international law, peace and war, justice and property, laws and the obedience they command, the duty of helping individual citizens in their need and co-operating with all to secure the prosperity of the State, both in the natural and the supernatural order. If these precepts were religiously and inviolably observed in private life and public affairs, and in the duties of mutual obligation between nations, nothing else would be required to secure mankind that "peace of Christ in the Kingdom of Christ" which the world so ardently longs for. It is therefore to be wished that the teaching of Aquinas, more particularly his exposition of international law and the laws governing the mutual relations of peoples, became more and more studied, for it contains the foundations of a genuine "League of Nations."

His eminence in the learning of asceticism and mysticism is no less remarkable; for he brought the whole science of morals back to the theory of the virtues and gifts, and marvellously defined both the science and the theory in relation to the various conditions of men, both those who desire to live the common everyday life and those who strive to attain Christian perfection and fulness of spirit, in the active no less than in the contemplative life. If anyone, therefore, desires to understand fully all the implications of the commandment to love God, the growth of charity and the conjoined gifts of the Holy Ghost, the differences between the various states of life, such as the state of perfection, the religious life and the apostolate, and the nature and value of each, all these and other articles of ascetical and mystical theology, he must have recourse in the first place to the Angelic Doctor.

Everything he wrote was securely based upon Holy Scripture and that was the foundation upon which he built. For as he was convinced that Scripture was entirely and in every particular the true word of God, he carefully submitted the interpretation of it to those very rules which Our recent Predecessors have sanctioned, Leo XIII in his Encyclical *Providentissimus Deus* and Benedict XV in his Encyclical *Spiritus Paraclitus*. He laid down the principle "The chief Author of Sacred Scripture is the Holy Ghost. . . . But man was the instrumental author" (*Quodlib.*, vii, 14, ad 5), and would not allow the absolute historicity of the Bible to be doubted; but on the basis of the meaning of the words or literal sense he established the fecundity and riches of the spiritual sense, the triple nature of which, allegorical, tropological and anagogical, he expounded with the most ingenious commentary.

Lastly, our Doctor possessed the exceptional and highly privileged gift of being able to convert his precepts into liturgical prayers and hymns and so became the poet and panegyrist of the Divine Eucharist. For wherever the Catholic Church is to be found in the world among whatsoever nations, there she zealously uses and ever will continue to use in her sacred services the hymns composed by St. Thomas. They are the expression of the ardent supplications of a soul in prayer and at the same time a perfect statement of the doctrine of the august Sacrament transmitted by the Apostles, which is pre-eminently described as the Mystery of Faith. If these considerations are borne in mind as well as the praise bestowed by Christ Himself to which We have already referred, nobody will be surprised that St. Thomas should also have received the title of the Doctor of the Eucharist.

The following very relevant conclusions may be drawn from all that has gone before. Let Our young men especially consider the example of St. Thomas and strive diligently to imitate the eminent virtues which adorn his character, his humility above all, which is the foundation of the spiritual life, and his chastity. Let them learn from this man of supreme intellect and consummate learning to abhor all pride of mind and to obtain by humble prayer a flood of divine light upon their studies; let them learn from his teaching to shun nothing so sedulously as the blandishments of sensual pleasure, so that they may bring the eyes of the mind un-dimmed to the contemplation of wisdom. For he confirmed by his precept, as We have said, his own practice in life: "To abstain from the pleasures of the body so as to be certain of greater leisure and liberty for the contemplation of truth is to act in conformity with the dictates of reason" (II–II, clvii, 2). Wherefore we are warned in Holy Scripture: ". . . wisdom will not enter into a malicious soul, nor dwell in a body subject to sins" (*Wisdom,* i, 4). If the purity of Thomas therefore had failed in the extreme peril into which, as we have seen, it had fallen, it is very probable that the

Church would never have had her Angelic Doctor.

Inasmuch, therefore, as We see the majority of young men, caught in the quicksands of passion, rapidly jettisoning holy purity and abandoning themselves to sensual pleasures, We instantly exhort you, Venerable Brethren, to propagate everywhere, and particularly among seminarians, the society of the *Angelic Militia* founded under the patronage of Thomas for the preservation and maintenance of holy chastity and We confirm the privileges of pontifical indulgences heaped upon it by Benedict XIII and others of Our Predecessors. And that the Faithful may be persuaded the more eagerly to enrol in this Militia, We grant members of it the privilege of wearing instead of a cord a medal round the neck impressed on the obverse with a picture of St. Thomas and the Angels surrounding him with a girdle and on the reverse a picture of Our Lady, Queen of the Most Holy Rosary.

But inasmuch as St. Thomas has been duly proclaimed patron of all Catholic schools because he marvellously combined both forms of wisdom, the rational and the divinely inspired, because he had recourse to prayer and fasting to solve the most difficult problems, because he used the image of Christ crucified in place of all books, let him be a model also for seminarians, so that they may learn how to pursue their studies to the best advantage and with the greatest profit to themselves. Members of religious communities should look upon the life of St. Thomas as upon a mirror; he refused even the highest dignities offered to him in order to live in the practice of the most perfect obedience and to die in the sanctity of his profession. Let all the Faithful of Christ take the Angelic Doctor as a model of devotion to the august Queen of Heaven, for it was his custom often to repeat the "Hail Mary" and to inscribe the sweet Name upon his pages, and let them ask the Doctor of the Eucharist himself to inspire them with love for the divine Sacrament. Priests above all will be zealous in so doing, as is only proper. "For Thomas was accustomed, unless prevented by illness, to say Mass daily and heard another Mass said by his *socius* or some other friar which he very often served," declares the careful historian of his life. But could anyone find words to express the spiritual fervour with which he said Mass himself, the anxious care with which he made his preparation, the thanksgivings he offered to the divine Majesty after he had said it?

Again, if we are to avoid the errors which are the source and fountain-head of all the miseries of our time, the teaching of Aquinas must be adhered to more religiously than ever. For Thomas refutes the theories propounded by Modernists in every sphere, in philosophy, by protecting, as We have reminded you, the force and power of the human mind and by demonstrating the existence of God by the most cogent arguments; in dogmatic theology, by distinguishing the supernatural from the natural order and explaining the reasons for belief and the dogmas themselves; in theology, by showing that the articles of faith are not based upon mere opinion but upon truth and therefore cannot possibly change; in exegesis, by transmitting the true conception of divine inspiration; in the science of morals, in sociology and law, by laying down sound principles of legal and social, commutative and distributive, justice and explaining the relations between justice and charity; in the theory of asceticism, by his precepts concerning the perfection of the Christian life and his confutation of the enemies of the religious orders in his own day. Lastly, against the much vaunted liberty of the human reason and its independence in regard to God he asserts the rights of primary Truth and the authority over us of the Supreme Master. It is therefore clear why Modernists are so amply justified in fearing no Doctor of the Church so much as Thomas Aquinas.

Accordingly, just as it was said to the Egyptians of old in time of famine: "Go to Joseph," so that they should receive a supply of corn from him to nourish their bodies, so We now say to all such as are desirous of the truth: "Go to Thomas," and ask him to give you from his ample store the food of substantial doctrine wherewith to nourish your souls unto eternal life. Evidence that such food is ready to hand and accessible to all men was given on oath at the hearing of the case for the canonization of Thomas himself, in the following words: "Innumerable secular and religious masters flourished under the lucid and limpid teaching of this Doctor, because his method was concise, clear and easily followed . . . even laymen and persons of little instruction are eager to possess his writings."

We desire those especially who are engaged in teaching the higher studies in seminaries sedulously to observe and inviolably to maintain the decrees of Our Predecessors, more particularly those of Leo XIII (the Encyclical *Aeterni Patris*), and Pius X (the Motu Proprio *Doctoris Angelici*) and the instructions We Ourselves issued last year. Let them be persuaded that they will discharge their duty and fulfil Our expectation when, after long and diligent perusal of his writings, they begin to feel an intense devotion for the Doctor Aquinas and by their exposition of him succeed in inspiring their pupils with like fervour and train them to kindle a similar zeal in others.

We desire that lovers of St. Thomas—and all sons of the Church who devote themselves to higher studies should be so—be incited by an honourable rivalry in a just and proper freedom which is the life-blood of studies, but let no spirit of malevolent disparagement prevail among them, for any such, so far from helping truth, serves only to loosen the bonds of charity. Let everyone therefore inviolably observe the prescription contained in the Code of Canon Law that "teachers shall deal with the studies of mental philosophy and theology and the education of their pupils in such sciences according to the method, doctrine and principles of the Angelic Doctor and religiously adhere thereto"; and may they conform to this rule so faithfully as to be able to describe him in very truth as their master. Let none require from another more than the Church, the mistress and mother of all, requires from each: and in questions, which in Catholic schools are matter of controversy between the most reputable authorities, let none be prevented from adhering to whatever opinion seems to him the more probable.

Therefore, as it behoves the whole of Christendom worthily to celebrate this centenary—because in honouring St. Thomas something greater is involved than the reputation of St. Thomas and that is the authority of the teaching Church—We desire that such celebration shall take place throughout the world from the 18th July until the end of next year wherever seminarians are in regular course of

instruction, that is to say not only among the
Preaching Friars, an Order which, in the words of
Benedict XV, "must be praised, not so much for
having been the family of the Angelic Doctor, as
for having never afterwards departed so much as a
hair's breadth from his teaching" (*Acta Ap. Sedis,*
viii, 1916, p. 397), but among other religious communities also, and in all seminaries and Catholic
colleges and schools to which he has been appointed
for heavenly patron. It is only proper that this
Eternal City in which Aquinas was once master of
the Sacred Palace should take the lead in holding
such celebrations and that the Pontifical Angelical
College, where St. Thomas may be said to be at
home, and the other academies in Rome for the
education of priests set the example in these holy
rejoicings.

In virtue of Our Apostolic power and for the
purpose of increasing the splendour and profit to be
derived from this celebration, We grant the following privileges:

1. That in all churches belonging to the Order
of Preachers and in all other churches or chapels to
which the public has or may have access, more particularly in seminaries, colleges or other institutions
for the education of priests, prayers may be said for
three or eight or nine days with the pontifical indulgences attaching to them which customarily at-

tach to prayers said in honour of the saints and the blessed;

2. That in the churches of the Friars and the Sisters of St. Dominic the faithful may once on any day they choose in the course of the centenary celebrations, after duly confessing their sins and receiving Holy Communion, obtain a plenary indulgence *toties quoties* they pray before the altar of St. Thomas;

3. That in churches of the Order of St. Dominic, priests, members of the Order or tertiaries, may, in the course of the centenary year on any Wednesday or the first free day of the week, celebrate Mass in honour of St. Thomas, as on his feast-day, with or without the *Gloria* and the *Credo,* according to the ritual of the day, and obtain a plenary remission of sins; those present at any such Mass may also obtain a like indulgence on the usual conditions.

In addition, a disputation shall be held in seminaries and other institutions for the education of priests on some point of philosophy or other important branch of learning in honour of the Angelic Doctor. And that the festival of St. Thomas may be kept in future in a manner worthy of the patron of all Catholic schools, We order it to be kept as a holiday and celebrated not only with a High Mass, but also, at any rate in seminaries and among religious communities, by the holding of a disputation as aforesaid.

Finally, that the studies to which Our young people devote themselves may, under the patronage of Aquinas, daily yield more and more fruit for the glory of God and the Church, We append to this Letter the form of prayer which the Saint himself was accustomed to use and exhort you to see that it be widely published. Let any person duly reciting it know that by Our authority an indulgence of seven years and seven quarantines is granted him.

As an augury of divine favour and in testimony of Our paternal benevolence, We most affectionately grant you, Venerable Brethren, and the clergy and people committed to your care the Apostolic Blessing.

Given at Rome at St. Peter's on the 29th day of June, the feast of the Princes of the Apostles, in the year 1923, the second year of Our Pontificate.

Pius PP. XI.

PRAYER OF ST. THOMAS

INEFFABLE Creator, Who out of the treasures of Thy wisdom hast appointed three hierarchies of Angels and set them in admirable order high above the heavens and hast disposed the divers portions of the universe in such marvellous array, Thou Who art called the True Source of Light and super-eminent Principle of Wisdom, be pleased to cast a beam of Thy radiance upon the darkness of my mind and dispel from me the double darkness of sin and ignorance in which I have been born.

Thou Who makest eloquent the tongues of little children, fashion my words and pour upon my lips the grace of Thy benediction. Grant me penetration to understand, capacity to retain, method and facility in study, subtlety in interpretation and abundant grace of expression.

Order the beginning, direct the progress and perfect the achievement of my work, Thou Who art true God and Man and livest and reignest for ever and ever. Amen.

Breinigsville, PA USA
28 August 2010
244439BV00006B/38/A